Cruising With Children

Cruising With Children

GWENDA CORNELL

ADLARD COLES
8 Grafton Street, London W1

Adlard Coles
William Collins Sons & Co. Ltd
8 Grafton Street, London W1X 3LA

First published in Great Britain by
Adlard Coles 1986
Reprinted 1988

Distributed in the United States of America
by Sheridan House, Inc.

British Library Cataloguing in Publication Data
Cornell, Gwenda
Cruising with children.
1. Sailing
I. Title
797.1 24   GV811
ISBN 0-229-11790-2

Printed and bound in Great Britain by
Mackays of Chatham, Kent

For Muriel and Erick Bouteleux

whose company made cruising with children so enjoyable,
whether in Barbados or the Bahamas, Miami or Maine,
in Tonga, Samoa and Papua New Guinea,
Bali and Malaysia

Contents

Contents

Contents

Acknowledgements

I would like to thank the following schools and organisations that have supplied me with information: Education Otherwise, National Home Study Council, Calvert School, Home Study International, Worldwide Education Service, the New Zealand and British Columbia Correspondence Schools and the American Community School in Cobham, England.

The Queensland Correspondence School deserve a special mention for the amount of material they have sent me and their positive attitude towards sailing families. Peter Evans of the Edward Grey Institute, Oxford, and Denis McBrearty of the Department of Anatomy, Cambridge, both gave me valuable information on dolphin watching. Dr Peter Noble kindly checked the chapter on health.

I am also grateful to my many cruising friends whose views and experiences I have quoted in the text and to Gill Stephenson for reading and commenting on the manuscript. Last, but by no means least, I wish to thank my husband Jimmy for his constant encouragement, valuable criticism and especially for providing the photographs.

1
The Starting Point

When we first started cruising with our two young children, it was a relatively rare occurrence to come across other families on sailing boats. Usually such encounters resulted in the children quickly making friends, while we parents swapped stories of how we coped with family life afloat. My initial reaction in taking children to sea had been one of trepidation and I had a lot of queries. How would I amuse them on passage? What if they fell ill at sea? Would they be seasick in heavy weather? Added to such questions was the major preoccupation of a cruise planned to last several years, the problem of their education. When we set out on our voyage, my daughter Doina was seven years old, my son Ivan five years, and we planned to cruise for three years. That we only returned to England six years later with a circumnavigation of 60,000 miles behind us and children of thirteen and eleven years old, is an indication of how much we enjoyed cruising life and how all my queries had been satisfactorily resolved.

A notable change in the sailing scene over these years has been the increase in the number of parents who now take their children to sea, not only for weekends or short cruises, but also on longer voyages and circumnavigations. In a survey carried out in the Pacific in 1984 among long distance voyagers, my husband Jimmy and I interviewed the crews of fifty boats and fourteen of these had children on board, ranging in age from six months to sixteen years. This was almost one third of all the boats, whereas in a similar survey undertaken five years previously, out of fifty cruising boats, only eight had children on board. Cruising has definitely become a family affair. This book is based not only on my own experiences, but also on those of the many friends I have made who were also cruising with children, as well as the long distance voyagers interviewed for

1

The author with her children watching dolphins as *Aventura* runs gently before the trade winds in the Pacific.

various surveys.

Undoubtedly there are problems and worries in taking children to sea, but they are not insurmountable and can be solved with some thought and careful planning. The same basic principles apply at sea as on land; it is only the watery environment that is different. Careful parents take precautions to avoid accidents in the home, whether from open fires, hot saucepans or flights of stairs, so it is only an extension of this attitude to take similar precautions on a boat. Few people would let a small child unsupervised near a busy road, without being convinced that the child knew his road safety drill and was aware of the dangers of traffic. Similarly most parents apply the same principle in not letting non-swimmers near water without some supervision or protective measure such as a lifejacket. Water safety has many parallels with road safety and, regarded as such, it becomes a matter of commonsense to teach one's child to live on or near the water safely. Far fewer children are victims of boating accidents than road accidents, and if they are taught water safety and can swim well the dangers are minimised even further.

In planning a cruise with children, the questions of safety, health, boredom, occupying children on passage and their education should be thought about with the same seriousness with which one tackles the questions of route planning or provisioning. Good or bad planning in this matter can have a major effect on the success or failure of a cruise. In this book I have tried to deal with most of the facets involved in cruising with children, and although the emphasis is on long-term cruising it applies equally well to those undertaking a short cruise or only day sailing. In short, it is for any parents who consider taking their children to sea.

Before looking at these aspects, possible problems and how to deal with them, I would like to consider the benefits in taking children to sea. For most children, life at sea has a positive effect on the development of their character and independence. Sailing is beneficial to children in many ways and parents who want the best for their children should be reassured by this. In our society today we are in great danger of making life too easy for our children. The kind of upbringing, in which no expense or effort has been spared, can sometimes result in a self-centred spoilt child with little concern for others.

There is a dilemma between not spoiling a child, yet at the same time not depriving him either of what is regarded as normal by the society in which we live. A certain amount of stress is necessary for every child's development, for being short of money or denied some desired item can help a child look outwards from his self instead of inward. Overprotection of a child can lead to a smothering of a child's personality, keeping him immature and preventing the development of his independence. Sailing is one way of providing some stress and limited hardship, although within a protective setting, which will help to build the child's character and teach him to depend on himself. A similar resilience has long been acknowledged to be induced by such activities as scouting, camping, mountaineering and canoeing, while the sail training ships and tall ships that take young people on extended cruises are also regarded as character building enterprises. There is a similar effect in family cruising.

It was thoughts such as these which contributed to our decision to take our children on a voyage around the world. I did not want my children to grow up taking too much for granted, to regard as necessities what were in fact the luxuries of life. I also hoped that by sailing they would come to appreciate the basic necessities, to learn that water does not always gush out of a tap at the flick of a wrist but might have to be transported in jerrycans from the shore in a dinghy.

The limited stress or deprivation that is involved in the sailing life does not in any way imply any cruelty or lack of love. Children are very resilient beings, even the tiniest, as was demonstrated during the 1985 Mexican earthquake, when small babies survived several days trapped under the rubble. Children are much tougher than we sometimes give them credit for and will adapt to new situations and environments often more easily than adults. This is especially so if they are surrounded and supported by a caring loving family.

The importance of the family and the influence of the parents are crucial to

A large boat like the Norwegian *Svanhild* is an ideal playground for the younger members of its crew.

the development of any child's personality. There has been a running debate over the years about how much heredity or environment contribute to a person's development. Yet even those who place all the major emphasis on what we inherit through our genes still acknowledge that the environment a child is brought up in has a considerable effect on that child's personality. The vital role played by the family is seen in many ways, as for example in the different ways many parents behave towards their sons and daughters, which affect their development as males and females. The continuous thread of events and experiences that take place throughout each person's life from earliest childhood onward, establishes the pattern with which the individual deals with later events and experiences. Human growth is cumulative and those children who interact early with a stimulating environment have the most substance to build on as they grow up. Most educationalists are now agreed that to produce the maximum rate and extent of intellectual development, it is necessary to provide the widest range of stimulating experiences.

It is fairly obvious that being on a boat at sea is a vastly different environment to living ashore. One of the most striking differences about living on a boat is that fathers are usually much more involved with their children and their upbringing than they are ashore. This stronger role played by the father invariably has a positive effect on his relationship with the children. Living in the confines of a small boat, family life is of necessity a closer affair than on shore, maybe more in parallel with life on a farm where the whole family have to cooperate with each other to keep the farm running smoothly.

As Liz Macdonald, mother of Jeff, who circumnavigated on 31 foot *Horizon*, explained to me, 'At sea, my son saw his father Bruce actually working, coping with problems under stress, such as when gear broke in heavy weather. Before we went sailing he only saw his father for a short time at the end of each day when Bruce was tired after a day's work. Now Jeff has more respect for his father and a much stronger relationship.'

This closeness of family life and the relationship many sailing children have with their parents arises out of the fact that the child often witnesses a parent dealing with a difficult problem or even an emergency. In a squall or bad weather, a child will have to learn that the safety of the boat, and thus ultimately the safety of the family, has to take precedence over other more minor demands or fears of the child. Learning to show patience, that getting the sail down quickly is more important than whatever the child's needs are, can lead to the child considering the needs of others as well as himself.

Fear in a child is often instilled by an adult: it does not always occur naturally. Small babies have little fear of water, for example, and can be taught to swim at a young age if that fear is never promoted. Adults do not always realise that they are conveying their fears through their behaviour, for the sensitive antennae of children can pick up more than mere words. The power that can be unleashed by Nature, such as during a storm, can be frightening for anyone, let alone a child; yet if adults do not panic but act calmly in such a situation, this has an enormous influence on a child, helping him to learn to face fear and danger calmly. This is a very important aspect to help develop in a child, for panic is the cause of many accidents.

On a boat, one of the biggest environmental influences is undoubtedly Nature herself. It is almost impossible to live on the sea without coming to respect the tremendous power and force of wind and wave. Living so close to the sea, however, a child can equally wonder at the beauty of Nature in its many changing faces. By being aware of the weather, how quickly it can change, how small one is compared to the vastness of the ocean, the marine environment can stimulate a child considerably and affect his thoughts and behaviour.

When I think about all the many children I have met on long distance cruising boats, the most striking similarity between them is their independence, confidence in themselves and self-sufficiency, as compared to many children living ashore. This independence coupled with an ability to express their own opinions is the hallmark of sailing children. Part of this comes from spending time in an adult environment, but it is also due to the special features of sailing life.

Seagoing children usually make friends very rapidly, both among other boats

Friends from other cruising boats celebrate Ivan's birthday at the Royal Suva Yacht Club in Fiji.

and on shore. It always amazes me how quickly children learn to make friends, for they seem to communicate with each other more directly and simply than adults, without the hang-ups acquired over a lifetime. The friendships they make with other seagoing children have a special quality, which cuts across nationality or culture, as the similar aspects of their life outweigh the dissimilar. Equally the cruising child will often have a chance to meet children of other races, religions and languages in those children's own home environments, which is very different from meeting visitors or immigrants back home, who are often separated from their normal way of life. My children soon came to learn that children are the same the whole world over; together they laughed at the same jokes and played the same games, whether cat's cradle, hopscotch or tipping each other out of a canoe. This whole expansion of a child's world that cruising brings, both at sea and in the places visited, can only broaden a child's outlook on life.

Being a family unit, a social entity that most societies recognise, makes a difference to travelling. Without doubt it coloured our own voyage. Sailing with children on board made our reception warmer in many places, especially in the islands of the Pacific, where children are regarded with special affection. Nearer home in the Mediterranean our cruising was often made more enjoyable by the presence of our children, as during our stay in the small port of Gela in Sicily. It was Ivan's sixth birthday, and sailing along the coast of Sicily bad weather

Doina in a dugout canoe with newly made friends on Rendova Island in the Solomons.

hampered our plans to reach our destination. As a birthday cake had been promised, we changed our plans and put into the small shallow port of Gela. There were no other yachts in the basin, only a medium sized motor boat, and while we were battling against strong winds to manoeuvre in, a man from the motor boat launched his tender, took our lines and helped us moor alongside him. We soon learnt that yachts rarely called at Gela and he soon learnt that it was Ivan's birthday.

'How far is it into town? Is there a bus?' asked Jimmy, explaining that he wanted to buy a birthday cake.

'Don't worry, I'll take you in my car,' said our helpful neighbour.

So without further ado we sped into town, stopping in the middle of the main street while the man and Jimmy went into the baker's shop. Telling the shopkeeper to refuse Jimmy's money, the man insisted on buying the biggest and most expensive cake in the shop as well as a mound of pizzas. Meanwhile a policeman was remonstrating with the children and me about the car being parked in the middle of the main road, to which we could only reply with what we hoped were explanatory gestures. As the man emerged from the shop, the policeman's face changed.

'Ah, Signor Pino – I didn't realise it was your car – no problem.' The policeman apologised to me. Pino nodded and drove off, taking us, the cake and the pizzas to his home.

'A young son must have his birthday celebrated in a proper fashion,' he told us, as he rounded up his own children and organised an impromptu party.

During our few days in Gela, we discovered Pino to have considerable influence: closed shops were opened on a Sunday for Jimmy to buy essential spares, the children were given gifts of fruit and other things. Over drinks in our cockpit, Pino discovered that Jimmy was a journalist. His face darkened and he frowned.

'I suppose you have come to Sicily to investigate the Mafia like all the other journalists?' he queried.

'Not at all,' Jimmy smiled at him brightly. 'I'm not in the least bit interested in the Mafia, only in sailing.'

Pino smiled back and winked at him. 'You are a very wise man.'

I have recounted this episode only to illustrate some of the enjoyment that cruising with children can bring. As with many aspects of life, a lot depends on one's mental attitude. If one expects to get fun out of cruising with children, one is much more likely to find that fun than if one regards children on boats as a bore. Still, there are many things to be considered before the fun starts and those I shall be examining in this book, from the safety and health of children on board to features in boat design that are relevant to cruising with children. Ideas for getting the most out of a holiday and practical suggestions for amusing children at sea have also been included. The second half of the book deals with the major problem of education afloat, although some of the suggestions made in this section may also be of interest to those planning shorter cruises. For simplicity, throughout the book the child is referred to as masculine, although there are just as many girls who enjoy cruising. What I would like to convey above all is that cruising with children can be enjoyable and is not so very difficult. As an additional bonus it can also be of great benefit to the children themselves.

So let's go cruising!

PART ONE
FAMILY LIFE AFLOAT

2
Boats with Children in Mind

Few people buy their sailing boat specifically with children in mind, yet if one has children and hopes that they will enjoy sailing for many years to come, it is worthwhile considering certain aspects of boat design before buying a boat. If one already owns a boat, the advent of children may simply necessitate a few alterations to make the boat more suitable for a juvenile crew.

A choice of boat depends on many personal factors: where, when and for how long one plans to sail, the age and number of the crew and always of course on the size of one's wallet. Yet whether planning Sunday outings to nearby bays or a circumnavigation, certain similar points should influence one's choice. The presence of children on board has to be taken into account whatever kind of sailing is done.

Size and space

One guiding factor is the age of the children, which governs not only the amount of space they take up, but safety and protective measures as well. Although babies themselves occupy little space, they can necessitate a lot of space-consuming items, such as carrycots or pushchairs – not to speak of piles of disposable nappies, very bulky items to store. For the Canadian couple Frances and Bill Stocks, their 30 foot cutter *Kleena Kleene II* was perfectly adequate for their cruising needs until the birth of their daughter Brandi in Papua New Guinea, an event not foreseen when they left British Columbia two years

11

previously. As we cruised in company to Indonesia, Sri Lanka and up the Red Sea, I watched their boat appear to shrink in size as the pile of baby paraphernalia grew.

We ourselves had left England with seven and five year old children happily established in the small forecabin of 36 foot *Aventura*, but by the time we were sailing in the Red Sea, Doina was a pubescent thirteen, not at all happy about sharing this small space with a teasing younger brother. A similar problem had befallen the Australian boat, *Warna Carina*, who had left home with three small children on board. By the time we met them in the Pacific several years later, on the last leg of their circumnavigation, they were accommodating three large teenagers and the family of five found their 36 foot boat rather overcrowded.

Growing children *do* take up space, often more than adults themselves, if one counts their toys, games and books. Therefore size and space are an important consideration in the choice of a family boat. Having sufficient space is also of prime importance in preventing the children getting on top of one, especially noticeable when one comes off watch tired or during bad weather. The question of size is so important that it may be worth considering buying a larger secondhand boat rather than a smaller new one if the money available is limited. I have never heard any parents cruising with children complain that their boat was too big.

When looking over a boat, it pays to envisage where the child or children are

Plenty of space is needed when friends come to play.

12

going to sleep and keep their playthings. If at all possible, the children should have a cabin of their own, preferably one you are able to shut the door on. It is very important for children to have enough space, where they can feel at home and have room to play. If it is completely separate then it does not matter too much if it gets in a mess during a passage, as this will not interfere with the running of the boat. Anyone who has come off watch at night and stumbled on a toy car or piece of building brick on the main cabin floor will know exactly what I mean. Even if a separate cabin is not available, a child should have some space for playing where a half-finished model construction or unfinished jigsaw puzzle could be left out. Even if one mainly daysails, a child is reassured by having his own bunk and territory, to which he always returns on each sail and where maybe he can leave toys from sail to sail. A contented child brings peace of mind for the parent too, so it is worth making some effort to achieve this.

On most boats, the forepeak is usually the children's province as this is conveniently out of the way and easily separated from the main accommodation. A few parents choose to designate another area for their children. When building his 40 foot *Iron Butterfly*, New Zealander Ian Hancock had cruising with his two sons in mind and allotted them the spacious aft cabin which had a large playing area, while the parents' own double berth was located amidships near to the saloon.

Cockpit position

Sailing with children may well influence the decision as to whether to have a boat with an aft cabin and central cockpit or not. An aft cabin gives some privacy to both adults and children alike, an important factor to be borne in mind. We certainly found our aft cabin a boon, as a place to retire to in order to read or sleep undisturbed when the children were playing noisily in the main cabin. Also, when the children were doing their schoolwork, Jimmy could work at his typewriter in the after cabin without either of them disturbing the other. If the cruise is going to be prolonged enough for schoolwork to have to be done, a quiet corner conducive to study should be considered. After eight years of cruising, which included a circumnavigation, the van Zelderens of *White Pointer* found it necessary to separate their two teenage children when they were studying in order to prevent them distracting each other.

If there is an after cabin, an interior throughway is much safer when small children are on board, as this means they can get into the rear cabin without having to go through the cockpit. This was a safety aspect which we did not have on our boat and the danger of a small child coming out into the cockpit was brought home to us after one sleepwalking episode at sea, fortunately when an adult was on watch. After that, in port we rigged up a bucket that clattered down noisily when the companionway doors to the cockpit were opened. This signalled to us sleeping in the after cabin that a child had come out into the cockpit.

Many parents choose a central cockpit as they feel this has more protection for small children. Our central cockpit on *Aventura* was not only deep, but was further protected by a wheelhouse, which meant that when sitting in the front corner of the cockpit the children could see out, but at the same time were sheltered from wind or rain. Whether the cockpit is in a central position or aft, the most important factor is that it is spacious, deep and well protected, especially when smaller children are on board. A raised coaming around an aft cockpit might be a design point to favour. Ideally the cockpit should be difficult for a child to fall out of. The Hantels of *Pytheas*, cruising with two young boys, had built up the sides of their cockpit so that it was very difficult for the boys to get out on deck while at sea. Another method of increasing protection is to fix canvas spray dodgers either side of the cockpit and across the stern if the design of boat features a more exposed aft cockpit. This will also help to protect a child against cold winds and exposure to the weather. Other protective measures will be discussed in the chapter on safety, which follows.

Hull form and rig

There are various points to bear in mind when considering hull form and rig. The fact that multihulls heel over less while sailing influences some parents, who feel that their children might come to enjoy sailing more quickly if they are upright. Multihulls have the further advantage of spaciousness for family cruising, although they are limited in not being able to carry so much weight. The weight capacity may be a problem for those planning to cruise further afield when the amount of water, fuel and stores to be carried is greater.

The factor of heel could also influence those who prefer to sail in a monohull to choose a stiffer boat which does not heel too much or too easily. This may mean sacrificing some speed in exchange for greater comfort. The amount of heel can make a large difference, not only to feelings of seasickness, but to games and toys staying put, not continually sliding up and down a surface when a child is playing.

The choice of the rig should be considered if children are older and keen to be involved in the sailing of the boat. Even if they are not yet old enough, a parent planning to keep a boat for some time should take into account that children might well wish to sail the boat when they do become older, and indeed should be encouraged to do so. Any of the rigs that feature a divided sail plan or smaller sails will be more easily handled by a child than a tall masted boat with large sails. This could indicate the choice of a ketch or yawl where the mizzen sail is small enough to be raised by a fairly young child. Alternatively if a single masted boat is prefered, a cutter with a staysail might be more manageable by a younger crew than a sloop.

Children enjoy being occupied around the boat, whether taking a turn at the helm, sail handling or tailing jib sheets. If they are not able to do these things because the boat is more of a racing machine, they can quickly become bored and frustrated with sailing. Whether the boat has a wheel or a tiller, it is worth considering if the boat can be steered by a child, particularly as regards visibility from the steering position. I have stood at the wheel of quite a few boats where, as an average height female, I was not able to see forward over the cabin roof easily, while a child would have seen nothing at all. A family boat should be able to be sailed by most members of the family, especially older children, and not only by the tall males on board. Similarly one can look at the winches to see if they can be operated by someone with less muscle power. In this respect self-tailing winches that can be operated with two hands might be an advantage for a young crew.

On deck

With small children on board the whole aspect of deck safety has to be considered carefully and is a function of the design. Wide side decks with high toe rails are obviously ideal where these small fry are concerned, the higher toe rail stopping toys and other little items from slipping off the side deck, as well as being safer for the children themselves. Tracks and other deck fittings should be in a position where they are not easily tripped over. Grabrails in convenient places on the coachroof are another point to look for. Many small alterations can easily be made by parents to their existing boats to improve safety for young children, such as easily reached grabrails. Canvas dodgers around the cockpit area and strong netting strung along sturdy lifelines are common measures taken by parents anxious to keep their young ones inboard. On some production boats parents have replaced the standard stanchions with higher than average ones. Laced with netting these are then taller than most toddlers, too high to be easily climbed over, and provide an effective safety barrier.

The sturdiness of pulpits, pushpits, stanchions and lifelines are other points to look for, all features which should provide something solid to hold on to when moving around the deck. If there is a gate in the lifelines, this should be checked to see if it has some form of safety clip and cannot be opened accidentally by small prying fingers.

If one is going to be getting on or off a boat with a child in one's arms or with a baby in a carrycot, it is worthwhile giving some thought to how this manoeuvre will be done. A gate in the lifelines may be one way of easing the

The sugar scoop stern on *El Djezair* was added later to the original design in order to make boarding safer and easier.

transfer of child or baby. A high freeboard on a boat can make the operation quite perilous and such boats are often difficult to climb on board from a dinghy. One solution is to have a ladder built on the stern. An increasing number of boats now have platforms or skirts at the stern and two families with children that I met in the Pacific had both recently added a sugar scoop skirt onto their existing boats. Not only does a sugar scoop transom make an excellent platform for swimming from and getting aboard from the dinghy, but one of these fathers specifically mentioned to me that he had added the skirt as a safety factor in case anyone fell overboard, making it easier to climb back on board.

Climbing in and out of hatches instead of using the companionway seems to be a universal childhood preference, so it is worth checking on how hatches open and if they can be secured properly when in the open position. It is all too easy to break the hinges of a hatch if this is not so. Many small modifications can be done on a boat to accommodate children; for example, we built a small wooden ladder onto the bulkhead next to the forward hatch in the children's cabin, with treads just wide enough to help little feet going up and down.

Interior Design

Companionway steps that are steep and narrow can be very hazardous to small children and in some boats it is a long fall from the cockpit into the boat. Ideally

16

steps should be wide and broad with handholds at the sides easily accessible to children going up or down. Similarly inside the boat it is easy to cast a glance around and see if the handholds and grabrails function at child level or not. If not, it is a comparatively simple matter to add some suitable grabrails at a lower level or to install handholds along the side of a navigation table or in a lower position in the galley.

Even with handholds available, small children are much more likely than adults to fall over, especially in a moving boat, in the same way that they fall and trip on land, moving too fast and not anticipating changes in movement. Imagine a child tumbling down the companionway steps and take a careful look at where the child could fall. In many boats there is a sharp corner of a navigating table or galley right in the way. The simplest solution is to take a plane and sandpaper and round off all sharp corners, especially any which may be at child height.

Similarly the position of the light switches should be looked at, especially in the children's cabin and the head compartment. Often these are too high for children to reach, being on the lights themselves – a point to bear in mind if one is building or fitting out a boat oneself. Any item that children ought to be able to reach on their own without adult help should be looked at from their point of view.

When I wander around boat shows and look at boats, the lack of good storage facilities has often struck me as one of the weaker points in boat design. The forecabin, which is often the children's domain on a boat, is usually poorly provided for in this respect. With children on board the need for sufficient storage space becomes even more crucial. Having a special place for everything goes a long way towards maintaining a boat tidy and ready for sea, so that nothing can fly about if it becomes a bit rough. If one is building or fitting out a boat oneself, it is fairly straightforward to plan enough lockers, shelves and cubby holes for a family's personal requirements, but even on standard production boats extra shelving or other storage provisions can easily be added.

Children do have a knack of acquiring lots of clutter, from toys and games to pebbles, shells or interesting pieces of driftwood found on a beach. One can be strict and limit their possessions, but the more things they are allowed to take with them, the better the chance that they will keep themselves occupied and happy. One solution is to limit the children's storage to their own area or cabin, which goes a long way towards preventing an overflow into the rest of the boat, even if it does sometimes result in a child sleeping on a bunk piled high with treasures.

Fitting out *Aventura* ourselves, we built a large number of lockers and cubby holes into the children's cabin in the fo'c'sle – not that that meant it was always tidy! Small fiddled shelves above their bunks held books, while a large triangular shelf was bolted into the forepeak, over the foot end of their bunks. This large

A removable triangular shelf in the forecabin of *Aventura* provides space for additional crew.

shelf was useful for holding larger items such as board games and soft toys and could be easily removed by undoing the bolts to get at the lockers beneath the bunks.

With proper storage, it is quite amazing how much can be carried on the average boat, and many cruising boats find room for such things as folding bicycles or a second dinghy, even if only a very small inflatable. Once the children have learnt to row, it is almost essential to have a second dinghy or one can easily find oneself marooned on a boat at anchor while the children have disappeared with the dinghy, always out of calling distance. A small sailing dinghy or sailboard will also provide much fun for youngsters, sailboards being usually stored along the side deck stanchions.

Deciding what to take and what to leave behind always poses problems and the only answer is to take as much as possible. Favourite soft toys are at the top of the list, providing comfort to children away from home. Books were another item that always loaded us down, although swapping books with children on other boats kept new reading material flowing for the same amount of storage space. Flippers, masks and snorkels are items that can be stored in a wet locker or a cockpit locker along with adult diving gear. Many children enjoy fishing, so fishing tackle is another item that might have to be stored; rods are not easy to find space for, although some people fix them along a cabin ceiling.

Babies and infants also increase considerably the demand for fresh water, for

Some parents even manage to find space for bicycles.

washing saltwater out of clothes or off tender skins is more important than with adults. The water storage capacity of a boat is another item to be checked when cruising with children. The amount of water carried can be increased if required by building in additional tanks or fitting flexible tanks into other storage areas. Alternatively extra jerrycans of water can be lashed on deck, some people choosing to do this anyway on a passage as a precaution for abandoning ship.

In conclusion, the design of a family cruising boat does not have to differ greatly from other cruising boats. Ideally a seakindly boat with features of adaptable space and plenty of storage capacity might suit most family requirements. Safety features should be well to the forefront of parents' minds as well as the protection offered in the cockpit. Size, rig, and cabin arrangement are all design features that might influence the choice of a boat, as does the age and number of one's children and for how long one envisages keeping the boat. From birth to adulthood spans a fair number of years and many people may well change their boat during this time to suit the changing needs of their growing family, the ideal boat for cruising with toddlers being very different to that which might be demanded by keen teenager sailors anxious for a boat with a faster performance.

3
Safe on Board

Many of the hazards for children on a sailing boat and the ways of preventing accidents are similar to those ashore, except that the presence of water adds a potentially dangerous element. In much the same way as one educates children how to cross the road safely, so afloat one has to teach them a safety code for behaviour on the water. Instead of road sense, one instils water sense.

The responsibility for the safety of infants lies solely with the adults on a boat, but this emphasis slowly changes as children grow up, until hopefully they become responsible teenagers able to be trusted to behave safely and sensibly on the water. Concern for a child's safety however, should not lead to overprotection, as this also has its dangers. In fact, the overprotected child is more likely to have an accident, because the child has not been taught how to protect and fend for himself. The aim should be to educate the child so that he is aware of potential dangers and knows the best way to avoid them. How one approaches teaching water sense will depend on the age of the child, but even the smallest child can quickly come to understand that there are certain rules that must be obeyed. Rules can help to turn certain ways of behaviour into habits, so that the child naturally and unconsciously avoids certain hazards. The reasons for a particular rule should be carefully explained to children old enough to understand, as they invariably act in a responsible fashion once they know the reason.

At sea

On almost every sailing boat I have come across, children were never allowed on deck at sea alone or unsupervised. This applied even to strong swimming teenagers, who took watches and handled sails. It is a simple rule to make, that an adult must give the go ahead before a young person leaves the cockpit. Confining children to the cockpit at sea is a sensible principle to follow, and asking an adult for permission to go forward can quickly become a habit. If the weather is at all unpleasant or the sea rough, it is most likely that children will prefer to stay below anyway and not even venture into the cockpit, let alone on deck. Rules and conditions about when and how children can go on deck are mainly a matter of commonsense.

As children are likely to spend time in the cockpit at sea, it is essential that the cockpit is well protected, an aspect which has already been considered in the previous chapter. Some form of cockpit protection is desirable, such as a spray dodger or spray hood. A permanent wheelhouse is ideal in that it enables the child to see what is happening all around without venturing into a more exposed position. In colder climates it is important to protect children from too much exposure to wind and spray, as they get cold very easily, especially when they are not moving about. In hotter climates a wheelhouse can also protect a child from the sun, which burns a sensitive skin so much more easily on water than on land. If there is no permanent protection, a piece of canvas can easily be stretched across the cockpit and tied to the rigging to give shade from the sun.

Harnesses

Although lifejackets may be kept on board for an emergency situation such as abandoning the boat, a harness is more convenient and less bulky for a child to wear at sea. Younger children and especially non-swimmers should wear a harness and be clipped on when they want to go forward. For older children a lot will depend on the sea and weather conditions, and in poor conditions they also should wear a harness.

Under our supervision our children have often been on the foredeck without a harness, especially once they could swim and in calm conditions, either to watch dolphins riding our bow wave, help change sails or have a refreshing cold shower from a bucket. In the latter case it is wise not to let a child lean over lifelines to fill the bucket, even if it is well tied with a length of rope. As the bucket fills with water it exerts quite a forceful drag, which can easily cause the child to let go of the bucket or even lose his balance.

While older children may wear a harness only when going on deck, for active toddlers, who are much more vulnerable because of their talent for darting about

21

quickly and unpredictably as soon as one's back is turned, the only solution is to make sure that they wear a harness and are attached even when in the cockpit. If the harness is attached to a central point, the child can move about freely to all corners of the cockpit. Preferably the line on the harness should be long enough to allow this freedom of movement, but not long enough for the child to be able to climb out of the cockpit.

For a harnessed child going on deck – and for adults, too, for that matter – a separate wire or line along the deck or on the cabin roof to attach the harness to is a good alternative to using the lifelines, where the harness has to be unclipped and clipped on again at each stanchion. One simple solution is to use a length of rigging wire, firmly attached at each end so that it lies along the deck. Another system which allows free movement right around the deck without unclipping the harness is the Latchway safety system. In this system, one of the standard lifelines is replaced with a stainless steel cable fixed by special fittings. The harness is attached by a line to a transfastener, which can move along this cable and cross these special fittings at stanchions or rigging without coming undone.

Often a child will learn to unclip the harness and move to the next section himself. We had no special provision for harness attachment on our boat and I became concerned at the agility which my young son soon showed in unclipping himself. While this may be acceptable for an older child, I think it is preferable that a harness cannot be too easily undone by a small child. The main reason for this is that if parents are under the impression that their child is safely harnessed, they may not watch quite so closely what the child is doing and so could be unaware that he has unhooked himself from the point of attachment. One way to circumvent this is by attaching the harness with a small shackle, which can be quickly undone by an adult but not by a small child.

The manner in which the harness is fastened is one point to look for when buying a harness for a child. Another aspect is the adjustability of the harness for size as the child grows. A harness should always fit a child snugly and not be too loose. On small toddlers the harness straps can easily fall off their shoulders and it may be necessary to sew the straps together at the back to prevent this. With the lack of suitable harnesses for the very young on the market, some parents have made their own by adapting conventional pram harnesses and reins. If extra security is desired for a smaller child, a strap of webbing can be sewn on to come between the legs to secure the harness in position. As the straps of most children's harnesses adjust to fit quite large children, the manufacturers should state a weight limit for the harness, ideally printed on it as instruction leaflets are easily mislaid.

Harnesses made to standard specifications have the tether line attachment point at the back of the harness so that the child will be towed face upwards in the water. However, if a small child falls overboard when the boat is not moving but at anchor, this could result in the child being suspended with his face in the water, so in these circumstances a front attachment might be better. The wisest course is to ensure that the tethering line is not long enough to allow the child to reach the water level at all. As children's harnesses are rarely provided by charter boats, this is an important item to take along if chartering or sailing as a visitor on a friend's boat.

In port

While at sea most parents are extremely vigilant, not allowing children on deck unsupervised or making sure they wear harnesses, in port there is a great danger of relaxing one's guard as, for example, when entertaining guests in the cockpit, and not paying full attention to what a child is up to. In fact, all the cases of drowning that I have heard of have occurred while the boat was at anchor or alongside a dock. The paramount rule for safety is that non-swimmers are never let out of one's sight unless wearing a lifejacket or harness, either on or off the boat, on a dock, or wherever there is water nearby. Undoubtedly the first priority for sailing children is that they learn to swim, and this is so important that I have made it the subject of a separate chapter.

Non-swimmers may have to be harnessed as described above in port as well as at sea, although this does restrict their movement and play. Understandably many children object to being tethered like animals. When we first met Muriel

It is not only afloat but also ashore that a young non-swimmer should be supervised or wear a lifejacket. What could happen if his toy car slipped off the dock into the water?

Strong netting on *Fiu* provides extra safety for little Madeli.

and Erick Bouteleux of *Calao*, their son Fabien was an energetic two year old. Erick had fixed a length of rigging wire along *Calao*'s wide side decks and Fabien spent hours running up and down the decks working off his energy, like a dog on a lead or a zoo animal pacing up and down to the limits of its cage. The other solution for the non-swimmer is a lifejacket or buoyancy aid and that is what Fabien soon progressed to, as his parents tired of the continual pounding up and down the deck. A lifejacket can be less frustrating to a small child than being tethered.

Safety on deck can be increased by various measures, such as safety netting or higher gunwhales and toe rails, all helping to keep a child inboard. The netting should be of sufficient strength to hold a child and be laced fairly taut. Such precautions will also prevent toys from falling overboard from the deck – doubly important, as trying to recover a lost object is one of the most likely reasons a small child might fall overboard himself. Some people think that netting gives a false security, and obviously netting should not abolish the need for careful supervision of non-swimming toddlers. Yet it is one more safety precaution to back up others, and I am of the opinion that one cannot have too many alternatives to ensure that children are kept safely on board. Impressing on the child that is forbidden to climb over the netting is also very necessary.

As small children so often run when others walk, it is important to ensure that the deck surface is non-slip. Teak is best left unoiled and unvarnished to avoid becoming slippery, while patent non-skid surfaces can be stuck onto other decks. If the deck is painted, a simple method to reduce slipping is to sprinkle clean fine sand onto the wet painted surface. When dry, the excess sand can be brushed off and another layer of paint applied to fix the sand in.

Various rules can be made to lessen the chances of slipping, such as not running on deck and always keeping the feet flat. Similarly leaning over the netted lifelines for whatever reason should be banned. Children are more surefooted with their feet bare, although this has to be balanced against them stubbing their toes on any objects protruding at deck level. Checking the decks for any such hazards and keeping them clear of clutter will lessen this risk. Obviously the wearing of shoes will be governed by the climate and temperature, and any shoes worn on deck should have a suitable non-slip sole, such boating shoes now being made in quite small sizes.

Careful parents might equally well make some rules for themselves too, such as not having music or a radio on too loud when a small child is playing out of sight, so that a child's cries would not be masked by excessive noise. When boats are rafted together these smaller children must be discouraged from climbing and jumping across to another boat, sometimes difficult to enforce when they see adults and older children doing this.

Madeli Curt, eighteen months old, shows off her lifejacket, essential protection for the young non-swimmer when not being supervised.

Lifejackets and buoyancy aids

There can be no hard and fast rules for when a child should wear a lifejacket or buoyancy aid, but parents should use their commonsense, mainly considering how unsupervised or far from help the child might be and his swimming ability. For the non-swimmer, wearing a lifejacket on deck or on the dockside should be as automatic as putting on a seatbelt in a car. Under certain conditions children who can already swim might also be advised to wear some form of buoyancy aid.

Anything that is designated as a lifejacket should be able to support the child on his back with his face well clear of the water. A lifejacket should also turn a child over onto his back if he falls into the water face down or is unconscious. Any jacket that does not meet these basic requirements should not be called a lifejacket but a buoyancy aid. Because of these requirements a lifejacket has all its buoyancy on the chest and can be bulky and uncomfortable to wear for a long period, restricting play and, in hot humid climates, irritating tender skins. For children who can swim or are beginning and can at least keep themselves afloat, buoyancy aids might be considered instead. As the name implies, these are only an aid to keep a child afloat, not a lifejacket, but some of the better ones come very close to fulfilling lifejacket requirements.

There are various points to bear in mind when selecting a lifejacket for an infant or a child. For the very young it is essential that the jacket has some permanent buoyancy and does not rely on inflation by mouth or by a bottle of CO_2 gas. Some jackets have part permanent buoyancy and rely partly on mouth inflation, so if this is the case the jacket should be fully inflated when it is put on, for a child cannot be expected to blow up a jacket in the water even partially.

The permanent buoyancy of a jacket is provided either by small air-filled pockets or by foam, of either the open or closed cell type. The air-filled pockets run the risk of being punctured or chewed into, but if these are sufficiently small and numerous the loss of one or two pockets may not make a large difference to overall buoyancy. Lifejackets with large air pockets or those that depend on mouth inflation can both be rendered useless if punctured and are very vulnerable to damage, for example by chewing. The non-return valve on inflatable jackets has also been known to have been chewed off and the inflation tube similarly damaged. This possibility of damage by chewing cannot be ignored when selecting a lifejacket for the young, as it is a natural reaction for many young children especially when in distress. Some jackets contain kapok or an open cell foam in sealed compartments and both of these forms of buoyancy can absorb water if their covering is punctured. The most suitable form of buoyancy in lifejackets designed for children is that of closed cell foam, which is virtually indestructable and does not absorb water if the outer covering is damaged. The type of buoyancy of a lifejacket should therefore be ascertained before purchase. These particulars and also the buoyancy weight for which the jacket is designed

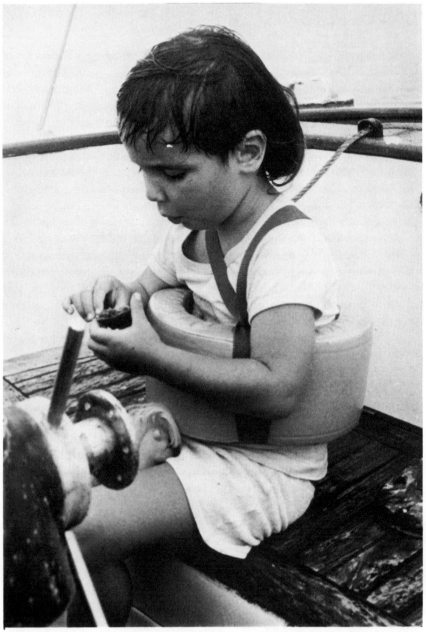

Three year old Luisa always wears her buoyancy aid when she is out on deck on *Abuelo III*.

should be available from the manufacturer and ideally should be printed on the jacket itself.

Buoyancy aids vary enormously in type and standard, some being jackets with permanent buoyancy of closed cell foam built in, while others consist of floats which tie around the body. The inflatable arm floats used in the teaching of swimming can also be considered as buoyancy aids. Again the most important points to consider are how much buoyancy there is, where it is, what it consists of and how it affects the performance of the aid. If there is not enough buoyancy on the chest, this will not turn the child over to lie safely with his face above the water. If the risk of the child falling in the water is slim, and the parent knows that the particular child is not likely to panic if he does – as in the case of a child who can swim a little and enjoys being in the water – a buoyancy aid may be a preferable alternative to a full lifejacket.

A garment for a baby must be of a type that fits the baby securely, so that he cannot wriggle out or turn around in it. One that fits like a jacket and fastens by zipping up the front with a strap between the legs to keep it in place is probably the best type. The major part of the buoyancy should be on the chest, so that the child floats face up. Some infant lifejackets have a hood or pillow padded with foam, which supports the baby's head. Similar jackets for toddlers have special flotation collars instead of hoods, which support the neck and head out of the water.

Most lifejackets for children are fixed by waist straps and webbing down the back with back buckles, designed to prevent the jacket riding up. However, many children find this type uncomfortable to wear. For this reason the waistcoat type of garment with a fabric back as used in some buoyancy aids might be preferable. Many of the jackets and buoyancy aids have crotch straps, although a few have garters or individual leg straps which children find more comfortable. Zips, simple buckles and clips are much easier to manage than ties or laces, especially for an older child who will be putting on the garment himself. Bright colours such as orange or red, which are easily seen in the water, are the first choice and some jackets have stripes of reflective tape to aid visibility. Another point to look for is that tightening of the waist straps can cause the garment to ruck into uncomfortable ridges. This will apply particularly to a slimmer child. Also the large collars of some jackets can flap about unpleasantly if it is windy. Jackets that are too long in the body can be uncomfortable when sitting in a dinghy, so a higher cut might be preferred.

It might be worth considering what the child will be wearing underneath the garment, and if there is room for bulky jumpers and jackets. Armholes large enough to take warm clothing might, however, let small arms slip out when the child is only wearing a swimming costume. Some parents require a child to also wear a harness under a buoyancy aid so if this is the case the ease with which the harness tether can be led out should be looked at. There is a limit, however, to the amount one can expect a child to wear for long periods of time and still enjoy sailing. A few buoyancy aids have a safety harness built in, which is a neat way to combine all requirements. The comfort of a lifejacket or buoyancy aid is of prime importance and will make a difference to how cooperative a child is in wearing it. In most family cruising situations a buoyancy aid is usually sufficient.

One way to feel confident about this decision is to test the aid on the child in the water. A child who is happy splashing about in the water with a comfortable buoyancy aid, or even only a swimming aid such as arm floats, can probably be left to play on a dock or boat at anchor wearing only that aid as a safety precaution without hindering his play too much. It is reassuring to test all lifejackets or buoyancy aids on a child, preferably in deep water, but failing that in a swimming pool or even in the bath for a small baby. This is the simplest way to verify that the jacket or buoyancy aid holds the child in the safe and correct position. A small child can also be given confidence this way if he realises that he will not sink when wearing the jacket, and this can help reduce the child's fear of water, increasing the chance that he will not panic if he should fall into the water accidentally.

Dinghy safety

Even after a child has learnt to swim, many parents insist on a lifejacket or bouyancy aid being worn in the dinghy, particularly in sailing dinghies or when the child is without an adult. Novice swimmers and younger children can go along with other children quite safely if they are lifejacketed. Almost without exception children afloat enjoy taking off in a dinghy independently to explore the little creeks and backwaters of an anchorage. At some point in their growing up, children have to be trusted to go off on their own and behave sensibly, and obviously this point will vary from child to child. It will also depend on where they plan to go, weather and sea conditions, state of the tide and how well they can row, sail or drive the outboard on the dinghy. The strength of the wind and any tidal currents must be carefully considered, so that there is no danger of the dinghy being swept away, because the child does not have sufficient strength to row against the wind or tide.

Most children enjoy learning to row and quite rapidly become proficient, even if sometimes unorthodox, rowers. It is worth spending some time teaching them a good rowing stroke, letting them practise while you are also in the dinghy or nearby until you are satisfied with their proficiency. Some small children find it easier to learn to scull with one oar as they can use both hands for this and so get more power behind their stroke than with an oar in each hand. My son taught himself to propel our dinghy quite fast by a one oared paddle stroke from the bows, which he invented himself. Even if normally rowing with two oars,

Non-swimmer Benedict Hantel (3) wears a buoyancy aid whenever he goes off in the dinghy with his elder brother Eric (7).

it is worth practising one oared propulsion too, for those occasions when an oar might be broken or let adrift. Rigid dinghies, whether made from wood, aluminium or fibreglass, are much easier to learn to row than an inflatable, and with children on board it might be worth ensuring that the tender is lightweight and easily rowed. Similarly a sensible eight or nine year old can manage a small outboard engine, provided he has been taught properly – again parents will make sure the child knows what he is doing before letting him out of sight.

If an outboard engine is used, needless to say, oars should always be included in the dinghy in case of engine failure. Similarly a bailer of some description should be carried in any dinghy, however it is propelled. If the outboard starts with a pull cord, some children may need to use both hands to pull it in order to raise sufficent force. As a safety precaution it should be a rule that passengers always turn their faces away from the cord being pulled. If the cord does not remain attached to the engine after it has been started, it should be tied onto something in the dinghy, such as the handles or seat, to ensure that it does not get lost. If they have a choice parents might be advised not to have the open-topped type of outboard engine, for an insufficiently pulled cord can flick back with the child's hand, or a girl's long hair could be accidentally wound in. The closed-topped engines where the starting cord retracts out of sight into the casing are to be preferred when being operated by a child. When an engine is used, the

31

danger of trailing anything in the water, such as towing a toy, should be emphasised as it could become entangled in the propeller. For the same reason making sure the painter is safely inside the boat should become a habit.

General dinghy behaviour for small children should begin with the rule of sitting still and not rocking the boat unnecessarily. Keeping feet and fingers inside is important especially when coming alongside a dock or boat. Not putting the feet or hands between the boat and the quay or dock applies not only to the dinghy but for all kinds and sizes of boats, as a sudden lurch or jolt can so easily crush fingers or feet. Never jumping into the dinghy and being careful not to push a dinghy away with one's feet as one clambers aboard a boat are other principles worth insisting on. Mastering the correct knots intrigues most children and they often become quicker and more adept knot makers than adults. This will ensure that the dinghy is always tied safely alongside or behind a boat or dock and will not come undone. For smaller children, tying both the bow and stern on short painters can make getting in and out of the dinghy easier. Nearly all the points about dinghy behaviour are commonsense, but it is worth pointing out the reasons for any rules, especially where outboard engines are concerned.

Getting on and off a boat from or into a dinghy can also be hazardous when carrying a baby or small child. The first requirement is for the dinghy to be tied firmly fore and aft so that it cannot move far away from the side of the boat. A baby can be carried either in a sling close on the chest, which is best for tiny babies, or in a carrier on the back, more suitable for the older infant. These baby carriers do leave the hands free for climbing on board, and if one is alone they are probably the best solution. For a two handed operation, there is the alternative method of transferring a baby to the boat in a solid carrycot on the floor of the dinghy and handing this cot up onto the deck, usually through a gate in the lifelines. The same principle is involved as in transferring boxes of stores or any such item, and the main danger is pushing the dinghy away from the side of the boat as one lifts the baby or child up to the other person on the deck.

The positioning of cleats on deck or the choice of fastening points for the dinghy will vary from boat to boat and everyone has to work out the safest way to board their particular boat, the height of the topsides being a crucial factor. Snaphooks fitted to the optimum length of line on bow and stern painters can make this operation quicker. Boarding ladders should always be firmly fixed so they cannot slide or shift about too much (this also prevents damage to topside paint). A skirt, platform or permanently fixed ladder on the stern was mentioned in the previous chapter on boat design, and these features do make boarding safer.

In the water

Most of the children brought up on and around boats turn out to be good swimmers, and those who sail in warmer waters are usually like fish, spending as much time in the water as on the boat. When they reach this stage many of the rules regarding lifejackets or dinghies obviously go by the board, as children play at capsizing dinghies for fun or deliberately fall over the side of the boat. Pushing another person who is not expecting it into the water, however, should always be discouraged.

Dangers in the water are the same for children as for adults and it is wise to make sure that children are aware of them. Attention should be paid to any undertows or currents that may exist where the children are likely to be swimming and they can be warned to stay away from obviously dangerous areas. Care should be taken to keep out of the way of fast speed boats and water skiers as soon as these engines are heard, for sometimes the drivers of such boats are not very attentive or aware of swimmers, particularly if they are snorkelling or under the surface. In many places there are strict restrictions about where one can water ski, yet occasionally I have seen water skiers weaving in and out of boats at anchor, regardless of children playing in the water. In one case the culprits were teenagers from one of the anchored boats, clearly having not been taught water sense by their parents.

A visit to an aquarium might be an easy way to show a child animals that are to be avoided if seen in the water. The excellent Suva Aquarium in Fiji has special displays arranged to show the dangers that lurk in the sea. Tropical waters appear to contain more such perils than temperate waters but, even so, poisonous animals are not all that common – no more than snakes, scorpions or tarantulas on land. One precaution that children can be taught is to be careful where they put their hands and feet, and especially not to put them into holes where they cannot see what is inside. Some creatures such as eels love to hide in dark holes and can bite if surprised.

From the moment they start swimming children should be encouraged to keep their eyes open underwater, and wearing a mask or goggles can help them to do this. Any creature that is not known or recognised should be treated prudently and with caution. Some of the most important animals to avoid are jellyfish of all types, stone fish, which lay motionless looking like stones on the seabed, and certain cone shells, which can release a poisonous dart. Large clams with attractively coloured tentacles can quickly shut tight over exploring fingers or careless toes and so should be given a wide berth. Prickly sea urchin spines are difficult to remove from feet and easily get infected if they are left – one of the reasons for wearing plastic sandals while reef walking, beachcombing or playing in shallow water.

It is, however, sharks that spring to most people's minds when they think of dangers in the water, although barracudas and eels can also give a nasty bite. In most anchorages or harbours, the possibility of sharks will be well known by local people and their advice should be sought. Fortunately the more dangerous sharks do not usually frequent enclosed lagoons and shallow waters but tend to stay on outer reefs and in the open ocean. Although not all species are equally dangerous and small lagoon sharks rarely take much notice of a swimmer or diver, sharks must always be treated very warily and certain rules must be obeyed in unknown waters. Sharks like to cruise where their dinner is, so they are usually to be found where there is plenty of fish. Swimming near any fish factory, processing plant or close to fishing boats where fish are being gutted should be avoided. For similar reasons any fish caught while spearfishing or with a net should never be carried near to the body but put immediately in a dinghy or on shore. Sharks feed at dusk, so that is the time of day to be cautious about swimming in unknown places; early morning or midday are much safer times. Another golden rule in shark suspected areas is never to dive or swim with a cut, wound or while menstruating, for blood attracts sharks, as does splashing or flailing about.

A general principle in water safety is to teach a child to stay calm and not panic if anything unusual happens. A panicking child is much more likely to come to harm and even drown as he gasps for air than the child who remains calm. Parental example is the key, for a parent who stays calm will generate confidence in the child too. Once while our children were swimming in a lagoon in the outer Bahamas, a shark appeared on the scene. It showed no interest in the swimmers, but of course Jimmy told the children to swim calmly to the dinghy and get in, while he stayed between them and the shark, holding his diving knife which he always wore strapped to his leg while swimming. This the children did without the slightest fuss or panic, because they already knew that splashing or making a noise might attract a shark more than normal swimming. They also knew that sharks rarely attack without first inspecting their prey, because we had discussed sharks and their habits with them when we first started cruising in tropical waters.

Inside the boat

Safety inside the boat has many parallels with safety in the home – for example, making sure that medicines are locked away or out of reach and that poisonous fluids or compounds are not stored in accessible places. Anything that could be poisonous should never be put into old lemonade or soft drink bottles.

A toddler will have to be watched all the time on a boat, not only to prevent injury to the child, but also to ensure that inquisitive fingers do not wreak havoc with expensive marine equipment. It is worth spending a few minutes looking around one's boat, maybe even on one's knees at child level, in order to assess what could be a hazard for a child. Where would a child be likely to fall from, the pilot berth or the companionway steps? A sensible rule to make is that a child never climbs up or down the steps with a toy in his hand, so that both hands are kept free for holding on. Are there any projecting corners in the fall path of the child? These can easily be rounded off, so that any fall results in bruises not nasty lacerations. How do the stopcocks in the head operate? Could an unwatched child accidentally flood the boat? Are there any moving parts in an accessible place on the boat that long hair or clothing could get caught in? These are some of the questions that might arise from looking around a boat from a small child's angle.

Whether one cooks by kerosene or gas, the cooker is one item to be particularly careful about allowing children near. Playing with the taps of a stove should be strictly forbidden, even if these are of the fail-safe variety. A turned on tap can easily release kerosene over the galley floor, while the danger of an explosion from released gas is very real. Although considering general safety inside a boat mainly in relation to toddlers, the correct use of bottled gas has to be learnt by all, young and old. The safest precaution is to always turn off the gas at the bottle as well as at the stove. This was the rule on our boat and it soon became second nature. The gas was turned off at the bottle and so the pipe to the cooker emptied of gas before being turned off there as well. In this way the danger of an explosion is minimised. Gas can be quite safe if used properly.

Saucepans should always have their handles turned away from the edge, so that a child cannot grab or pull a saucepan over. Saucepans with lug handles are much safer on a boat as the handles do not project. The top of the stove should be fitted with pan holders into which the saucepans fit snugly. When cooking in a seaway, it is safer to use the oven if possible and important to keep children well away from the pouring of any hot liquids. Children should be sitting down in a secure position when they eat so as to lessen the chances of them upsetting hot food over themselves. Young children should not be given too hot food; it is better to wait for it to cool slightly before serving it out. The only accident we had during 60,000 miles of sailing was when Ivan tipped a bowl of hot custard down his bare chest in his impatience to eat it. It might be better to serve such food in a mug with handles rather than in a bowl, if it is to be held in the hands and not eaten at a table. If a small baby or infant has to be fed, it is safer to do this with the child on one's lap so that parent and child move together with the movement of the boat.

Writing about accidents and safety always seems rather horrific, whether one is considering gas explosions, sharks or falling overboard. Yet similar dangers exist on land too, in the home or on the streets, and the most important point is to teach a child to be aware of these dangers and how to act sensibly to avoid them. Overprotection bears the risk that the child does not have a chance to become independent and think for himself, yet this should never be confused with valid protective measures which need to be taken. Making sure that a toddler who is unable to swim is never near water unsupervised or without a lifejacket is not overprotection, but very necessary protection indeed. I have often been impressed by how sensible sailing children can be, their independence and maturity often marking them out from their land based counterparts. Until they reach that stage, however, the smaller ones will require the utmost vigilance and in this field parental responsibility cannot be shirked.

4
Learning to Swim

One of the first priorities for any parents considering taking their children to sea or even near the water is to ensure that they can swim. It has now been well established that it is possible for babies to stay afloat even before they can walk, so no age is too young to begin learning to feel at home in the water. The accent in this chapter is on gaining confidence in the water and keeping afloat, drownproofing as opposed to learning swimming techniques or specific strokes. The aim is to ensure the survival of a child who accidentally falls in the water, not to produce an Olympic champion.

I have twice been in the vicinity when children drowned, one a sixteen year old non-swimmer who was fooling around on a windsurfer close to a beach, and the other a two year old girl playing unsupervised on a dock and not wearing a lifejacket. I am continually surprised at the number of parents who cruise with their children and who have not made the effort to teach them to swim at an early age. Among fourteen long distance voyagers interviewed in the Pacific who had children sailing with them, eleven out of the total of twenty children could not swim properly. These were mainly the younger children, some of whom were in fact in the process of learning. Only one of these eleven non-swimmers wore a buoyancy aid or lifejacket as a matter of course; two wore harnesses at sea but not in port, their parents claiming to be always vigilant, while another young non-swimmer only wore his lifejacket when his parents were not supervising him, for example when he was rowing in the dinghy with his elder brother.

I was amazed to be told that one of the non-swimmers, a six year old, had already been fished out of the harbour twice and still his parents did not insist

Mareva (4) and Jimmy (6) feed the ducks from the deck of *Vahine Rii*. With children who cannot swim one must be more careful in harbour than at sea.

on him wearing a lifejacket; nor did they appear to be making any effort to teach him to swim. In my mind this kind of attitude amounts to criminal negligence. Effort is the key word, because that is the main requirement needed: a frequent and regular effort has to be made by the parent, devoting time to the task in hand. In contrast to the example quoted above, on *Swan II*, further along the quay in the same harbour, Nicky Samuelson, also six years old, had been swimming since she was seven months old and at the age of three had even been offered a place in a junior swimming team – demonstrating the result that a little effort can produce.

Most of the progress in teaching the very young to swim has come from the warm climes of California and Australia, where garden swimming pools are commonplace and many parents fear for their toddlers' safety. Virginia Hunt Newman in the United States and Claire Timmermans in Australia are two of the teachers who have pioneered techniques for teaching babies to swim and both of them have written useful books on the subject.

Water babies

Babies are not born being afraid of water: this fear is only developed from adult behaviour and attitudes. In fact newly emerged from the wet and watery womb, babies are quite happy lying in warm water even from a few days after birth. The first steps in helping a baby to feel at ease in water can be taken at home in the bath tub on a regular basis, in clean warm water before any soaping or shampooing begins. The baby should never play in soapy water because this can get in his eyes and so make him associate water with unpleasant symptoms. Ideally once a day, but at least three times a week, a consistent programme should be followed, because regularity and frequency are important for a small child with a short-term memory. Professional teachers consider it even more effective if the parent actually gets in the bath with the tiny baby. Even with the youngest baby it is advised to use the normal bath tub and a reasonable depth of water, so that the child gets used to a larger volume of water.

The main principle is that water play should be fun, something to be enjoyed, which is not too difficult to convey to the normal child splashing and playing with his toys in the water. The first step is to start trickling water over a baby's head and face from a sponge, gradually increasing the amount over the eyes. Supporting him under his neck and holding one leg, the baby can be floated on his back, gently moving him backwards and forwards. The support given to the child can gradually be reduced over a period of time. When the baby is used to this floating, he can be moved so as to make waves, letting them ripple over his head from the top, not from the feet, so that water does not flow into his nose.

Also as a game the baby can be playfully dunked up and down in the water, blowing onto his face all the time as he goes under. The main purpose in this type of play is to get the baby used to having water over his face and not to mind. When this is achieved the baby can be submerged for an instant; by a natural reflex he will hold his breath. This submersion time can be gradually increased over the weeks until it lasts several seconds. The reason for blowing on the face until the child goes under is that this causes the baby to shut his eyes and naturally hold his breath. It also becomes a signal that he is about to go under.

When the baby is happy about getting his face wet, one can progress to holding him front down in the water encouraging him to kick and splash. Supporting the child under the chin and tummy, he can be similarly submerged for a few moments. Always make sure that both nose and mouth are either out of the water or both totally submerged, so that the baby will not try to breathe underwater, as might happen if either nose or mouth only are submerged. Another game is to blow bubbles into the water, babies learning to copy their parents quite easily. All of these exercises should be made into fun, and if a child is upset by any of them do not insist, but return again to the beginning and just play or trickle water. Never force a child to submerge if he is obviously very unhappy about it.

The next step is to lay the baby under the water on his front, supporting him under the chin and tummy and letting him kick his legs and paddle his arms as he will probably do instinctively. By slight pressure under the chin, the baby's

39

head can be brought to the surface so that he takes a breath. This is repeated often, so that pressing on or lifting his chin becomes a signal for coming up for air. All the time the baby should be encouraged and praised and the sense of enjoyment maintained.

Once the baby has gradually become used to submersion and water play in the bath, it is time to progress to a pool. This is where more effort will be needed, for finding a learner's pool that is both warm and shallow is not easy in many areas. A temperature of 26–32°C (80–90°F) is recommended for young beginners, and for small babies it should ideally be nearer 32° (90°C). Often public swimming pools are below this temperature, and if there is no alternative pool the lesson time should be reduced and the baby got out of the water into a warm towel quickly at the end of the lesson. Learning to swim in a warm climate has obvious advantages in that a suitable pool is more easily found. If no pool is available, continuing to play and submerge in the bath will still have an advantage in making a baby happy about water and will make swimming easier later on when the time comes.

For the first experience in a pool, the baby should be taken in gently held in his parent's arms and then the same kind of games that were played in the bath, blowing bubbles, dunking and splashing, can be gradually started. If the baby is laid in the water on his front and moved along, he will automatically make movements similar to those of crawling on land. To encourage the child to open his eyes underwater, some coloured non-floating toys or objects can be placed on the bottom of the pool and the child encouraged to search for them.

The main emphasis is for the baby to feel at home in, and especially under, the water. From then on, the amount of support under the baby can be gradually reduced and the submersion time increased. The baby should always be guided up by the chin to the surface in order to breathe, but this pressure can become lighter and lighter as the reflex of coming to the surface for air is established. The aim, eventually, is to release the baby completely under the water. Similarly the baby can be dunked up and down, again blowing on his face all the time until he goes under to encourage the holding of the breath. Some time should also be devoted to floating the baby on his back with his arms outstretched. Younger babies can often learn to float more easily this way than older babies, because over nine months or so a baby will become more interested in what else is happening all around him, and may wriggle, move his arms or try to turn.

No attempt to teach swimming strokes should be made and only the natural doggy paddle encouraged. This underwater method seems strange to many adults who learnt to swim in a different fashion, but it is the more natural method for babies, perhaps more akin to the womb they came from. The purpose is to waterproof the child, so that an accidental tumble into water will not automatically result in a gasping and panic-stricken child struggling to keep his head above water, which can in turn result in much more rapid drowning unless the child is speedily rescued. Proper swimming strokes and improvement in technique can be learnt in good time when the child is older.

Toddlers and infants

An infant can be taught to swim using the same techniques as described for a baby and can also begin by having fun in the bath with splashing, face-wetting and dunking under the water. Again the aim is for total submersion, the natural underwater method. In some respects it is a little easier once a child can talk and also understand verbal directions more readily, although the child might already have developed some aversion to water. In the pool, familiarisation with water can progress in the same way until a child can do a basic underwater doggy paddle and float on his back.

Before moving on to actual swimming the child must learn to breathe out underwater, because a baby or small child automatically holds his breath when submerged. This can be taught in the bath tub or in a bowl, as a game of watching the bubbles rise. In shallow water where the child can keep his hands on the bottom while his legs float on the surface, he can take a breath, submerge his face and breathe out naturally blowing bubbles. As well as in the bath, this can be practised in a shallow pool or even in the sea off a beach. If the seawater is warm enough, there is no reason why all of this learning cannot take place in the sea when a pool is not available.

Jumping up and down in the water while holding onto the parent's hands and eventually submerging, is another way of playing a game that gets a child used to submersion, encouraging the child to jump higher out of the water and sink lower underneath with each jump. Learning to jump from the side of a pool into the water towards a waiting adult also instils confidence.

Once the child has learnt to float unaided on his back, swim a rudimentary doggy paddle, and is happy about total submersion, able to keep his eyes open underwater and breathe properly, then teaching can progress to swimming on the surface and learning different strokes, using buoyancy aids such as float boards.

Older children

For children who have not learnt to swim early and may have developed some fears or apprehension about total submersion in water, the natural underwater method will probably have little success. In this case it may be better to begin teaching with the aid of inflatable arm floats or other forms of swimming aid.

Most arm floats are made of a plastic material, having two compartments which can be inflated separately. Fully inflated and pushed on the arms above the elbows, these floats will keep a child on the surface with the minimum of movement from arms and legs. They are ideal for giving the non-swimmer confidence in the water. An older frightened child can even wear two floats on each arm to give him the initial confidence that he is not going to sink under. The child should be taught to propel himself along by kicking his legs, on both his back and his front, and also be encouraged to float on his back with arms and legs outstretched. As the child learns to float and doggy paddle, the arm floats should be removed as soon as possible so that he does not become too dependent on them. This is best achieved by progressively deflating first one of the two compartments on each arm and then the second compartment. As the air is released a little more at each swimming session, the child's confidence grows as does his ability to move his arms in a better fashion without the hindrance of the floats. Once this confidence is established the arm floats can be finally discarded.

If a child learns to swim on the surface with the aid of arm floats, it is important not to neglect giving him underwater experience, so lots of face wetting, head ducking, blowing bubbles and opening the eyes underwater should also be included. This mental barrier of being unwilling to submerge completely and voluntarily is the biggest obstacle to becoming a true swimmer. If an older child has a phobia about submersion, one good way to build confidence is to practise immersion in a bowl containing only a few inches of lukewarm water. The child should get used to immersing his head, at first pinching his nostrils if he wants to and then progressing to blowing air out underwater and opening his eyes. When some confidence has been established using the bowl, he can try the same thing in the bath before progressing to trying it in a pool. The next stage is to help the child to float on his back and his front without moving his arms and legs unnecessarily. Once he can discover that he does not sink automatically, he will be at the point of overcoming his main difficulty in becoming a swimmer.

Drownproofing

The idea of drownproofing originated with Professor Fred Lanoue of the Georgia Institute of Technology. It is basically a floating technique for keeping alive in the water with the minimum of effort and can be taught to any children who are old enough to understand what is required. It is not necessary for them to be proficient swimmers to learn the technique.

The basic float position is on the front with the head submerged, the arms loosely forward and the legs hanging down. The majority of children will find that with their lungs full of air they have a natural buoyancy and can just hang in this fashion with no effort at all. In order to breathe, all that has to be done

Arm floats can be used as a buoyancy aid, as well as giving confidence in the early stages of swimming.

is to exhale into the water, still keeping the face down, then lift the head upwards out of the water by giving a little movement of the arms. A good breath is taken and then the face dropped back into the water. The cycle is repeated and, as the body is in a resting position using little energy, the person does not get so tired but can keep this up for a long time. The main reason for keeping the head down and submerged is that it is proportionately one of the heaviest parts of the body; a considerable effort is needed to keep its weight above the surface, so it is better to let the water support it.

In practice a major factor in survival, just as much as any technique mastered, is the temperature of the water. Although survival time is very short in cold water, in the tropics the sea is often at a temperature where prolonged survival is possible. A few years ago, sailing among the Gilbert Islands, the crew of a New Zealand catamaran fished out of the water a small girl who had been washed out to sea from a nearby island while fishing on the reef. She was semiconscious, but had survived two days in the water by naturally adopting a survival position curled up like an embryo. In many Pacific islands children have always been taught to swim as babies in similar ways to those outlined above. The catamaran took her back to a village already mourning her death.

In colder waters some insulation is provided by clothing trapping a layer of air, and beginners should not be encouraged to try to remove their clothes in the water. As wet clothing out of the water will weigh heavily and create a drag, they should be taught to keep all parts of the body that are covered by clothing underwater to help them stay afloat. Survival techniques, such as removing clothes, knotting ends of trousers and sleeves and then blowing the clothes up into bouyancy bags, which are taught by some swimming teachers, should only be practised by children who are already proficient swimmers.

Acclimatisation with lifejackets

If a child has not learnt to swim, but wears a lifejacket or buoyancy aid on the boat or while playing on a dock, it might be worthwhile putting the child into water out of his depth with this garment on, the parent remaining close at hand. Firstly, this will give the parent the reassurance that the aid is able to do the job it was purchased for and support the child in the water. Secondly, it will give the child confidence that he is not going to go under in deep water. It is important to do this in water where the child cannot touch bottom and an ideal place is around the boat while at anchor. This will help a child not to panic if he does accidentally fall in. Even after my children and their friends could swim well, they still sometimes chose to play in the water with their buoyancy aids on, lazily basking on the surface with the minimum of effort.

In very hot climates a full lifejacket can be very irritating for a small child to wear, especially a child with sensitive skin, and some parents use the arm floats as an alternative under these conditions. Again it is important to discover how the child behaves in deep water with the arm floats on, because these are only an aid to swimming and not a lifejacket. However if the child is happy and accustomed to being in the water with the floats on, these may be sufficient to save him if he accidentally slips off a dock or a boat while playing.

The emphasis in this chapter has been on making children safe in the water, not on any swimming proficiency. If a parent feels unable to teach his child, there are many professional teachers who make a speciality out of teaching the very young to swim. Yet most of these teachers agree that the parent is the best person to undertake the task if possible, because of the natural confidence that a small child has in his parents. The guidelines in this chapter are of necessity fairly brief and greater detail can be found in specialist books on the subject of teaching swimming, which are well worth consulting. Regular and constant effort is undoubtedly needed, but it will be well rewarded, because there is a clear peace of mind that comes when one's child is equally at home in the water as he is on dry land.

Books

Lanoue, F. (1963) *Drownproofing*. New Jersey: Prentice-Hall, Inc.

Newman, V.H. (1967) New York: Harcourt Brace Jovanovich and (1985) *Teaching an Infant to Swim*. London: Angus and Robertson.

Roy, H. (1972) *Beginner's Guide to Swimming and Water Safety*. London: Pelham Books

Timmermans, C. (1977) *How to Teach Your Baby to Swim*. London: Heinemann and New York: Stein and Day.

5
Child Health Afloat

Dealing with a sick child or coping with a medical emergency while away from professional help is a natural worry for parents thinking of cruising with their children. In some respect they may be encouraged, because a child is less likely to catch common infectious diseases on a boat than on shore. Nevertheless accidents can happen or a child can fall ill, and the wise parent will make some preparations for such an event. Even if one does not sail very far offshore, it may still be several hours after an accident before professional help can be reached, and some knowledge of what to do in an emergency can save a life or lessen injury. The most obvious case when immediate action is vital is when a child has stopped breathing after falling in the water. Those planning an extended cruise out of the range of normal medical assistance have to be prepared to deal with a much greater range of problems. Taking a short first aid course as part of the general preparation for cruising would never go amiss in dealing with both adult as well as children's emergencies.

The first step in allaying fears is to have a good book at hand. There are various first aid manuals available, some having been written especially for yachtsmen, such as Peter Eastman's *Advanced First Aid Afloat* or Dr Counter's *The Yachtsman's Doctor*. However, these books deal mainly with adult problems, although many of the essentials could also apply to children. St John Ambulance publish a delightfully simple and clear *The Essentials of First Aid*, which is used to train young first-aiders such as cadets, scouts and guides. I also had on my bookshelf *The Ship Captain's Medical Guide*, published by Her Majesty's Stationery Office, for merchant ships not carrying a doctor. This is a very comprehensive book packed with information, and although dealing with the problems of merchant seamen, such as drunkenness and venereal disease, it does have very clear tables for diagnosing the causes of abdominal pain, unconsciousness, or the differences between measles, German measles and scarlet fever. The signs, symptoms and treatment of all major diseases are clearly laid out so as to be understood by a layman. The book deals with many matters that particularly appertain to life at sea and in port, such as checking on the purity of water supplies. For the common illnesses and problems of childhood there are many manuals on child care written for parents.

Having bought a book, it is essential to look through it before consigning it to the bookshelf and particularly to read the sections on essential first aid. In an emergency it is usually vital to act quickly; there may not be time to wonder where one has put the first aid book or to thumb through the pages looking for the section that is relevant. Once the essentials have been dealt with, the book can be consulted at one's leisure for further treatment or procedures.

Immediate first aid

There are three major priorities in an emergency:

(1) To restore breathing.
(2) To stop major bleeding.
(3) To move the patient out of danger.

If a child has stopped breathing, it is essential that resuscitation is started immediately, even if the child is also bleeding or in an exposed position. Obviously if breathing has stopped due to immersion in water, the child has to be got out of the water first; but if, for example, the child has been knocked out by the boom and is lying unconscious and not breathing on the side deck, artificial respiration should be begun at once before moving the child into a safer place.

Stopped breathing does not necessarily mean death, but the brain can only function for a few minutes without oxygen before it is irreversibly damaged, so a delay in resuscitation may mean that, although a life is saved, the person can be seriously damaged mentally – in short, a vegetable for the rest of his life.

Mouth-to-mouth ventilation

(1) Remove any obstruction in the mouth and lay the child on his back. A small child can be held in the air by the legs to quickly let water or vomit drain from the mouth and lungs.
(2) Place one hand under the neck, the other on the forehead and tilt the head

47

back. Then move the hand which was under the neck to the chin and push the chin up in order to lift the tongue clear of the airway.

(3) Take a breath. For a small child, cover both the nose and mouth with your mouth and puff very gently. For an older child, pinch his nostrils, put your lips around his mouth and blow. In both cases pay careful attention to the chest rising.

As adults' lungs are much stronger and bigger than a child's, one must be extremely careful not to over-inflate and so damage the lungs. This depends on the size of the child, and is why it is essential to keep an eye on the chest as one blows gently.

(4) When the chest has risen fully, move your mouth away and finish breathing out.

(5) After the child's chest has fallen, repeat the process, but give the first few breaths in quick succession before the chest falls completely.

(6) Now check the carotid pulse in the hollow of the neck near the voice box – it is more reliable than the wrist pulse to ascertain if the heart is still beating.

(7) If the heart is beating, continue to give mouth-to-mouth ventilation until the child is breathing normally. It may be necessary to give partial help as the breathing recovers in gasps and starts. Keep an eye on the child's breathing for several hours afterwards.

(8) If the heart is not beating, begin chest compression. Children need less pressure than an adult, so place only one hand over the centre of the breastbone, press down about an inch (2.5 cm) and release, doing about fifteen compressions in about ten seconds. Then give a couple more mouth-to-mouth and nose ventilations.

For babies, use only two fingers over the centre of the breastbone and press less hard, about half an inch (1.5 cm).

Two people can work together effectively, one person doing the breathing while the other does the chest compression at the rate of 100 compressions and 20 breaths a minute; that is, approximately five compressions to each inflation of the lungs.

(9) Check the pulse every minute.

It is difficult to say how long one should continue if the child does not revive. There have been a few instances of children being successfully revived after several hours of resuscitation.

Once breathing has been restarted, other problems can be dealt with, although major bleeding can be stopped by a second person while mouth-to-mouth ventilation is going on. Bleeding can usually be stopped quite easily by firm direct pressure on the bleeding point with fingers or the palm of the hand. Even major bleeding can be halted this way. Pressure should be kept on the wound for five to fifteen minutes in order to give the blood time to clot.

Burns

Burns are a hazard on a moving boat, even if one is careful to keep children away from the stove and the pouring of hot liquids. During six years of living on board, a burn was the only serious accident we had, when Ivan tipped a bowl of hot custard down his bare chest. Being a thick viscous mixture, it stuck to his skin excruciatingly. Fortunately I knew what to do and, although a sizeable patch of skin was completely burnt off, not even a scar remains today.

The first thing to do with a burn is to immediately cool the affected skin area to prevent further or deeper damage. This can be done by plunging a hand or foot in a bowl of clean cold water (iced if possible) or by standing under a cold shower for ten minutes. Even cooling the area with buckets of clean sea water will do if this is more readily available than fresh water. The most important thing is to cool the skin. Once that is done time can be taken over further treatment.

If the burn is at all serious, there are two dangers: infection and the loss of fluid leading to shock. The entire burn area should therefore be thoroughly disinfected. Wash your hands and any instruments such as scissors in a disinfectant solution. Swab the skin area carefully with disinfectant and then

A few days after being burnt on the chest, Ivan sports a burn dressing held carefully in place, while assembling his train set on the aft deck for an audience in the Solomon Islands.

cover with a special sterile burn dressing. If the burn covers a large area, it may not be possible to cover this with a burn dressing, so place the child on a clean sheet and leave the burn open to the air after swabbing, making a tent over the child with another sheet so that no material comes in contact with the burn. If the burn is severe, start a course of antibiotic to prevent infection.

For the second danger of shock and fluid loss, give the child plenty of his favourite drink in small but frequent sips, for example several cups an hour, especially during the first hour.

Medical assistance should be sought urgently for any major burn, and if anything over 20 per cent of the body surface is affected it should be considered as a burn that can have lethal consequences if not properly treated.

I have dealt with the major emergencies first, because immediate first aid is of such importance. There are many other things which are equally important or serious, but they can usually be dealt with in a more leisurely manner.

Protection from disease

It is important to check that one's child has had all necessary vaccinations before leaving on a cruise. Children are normally immunised in infancy against various diseases, such as diphtheria, tetanus, whooping cough and poliomyelitis, and booster doses given at around five years of age. Immunisation against tetanus is highly recommended for anyone, child or adult, who is planning to sail extensively. Tetanus is a very unpleasant disease, with a high mortality rate, and any wound, such as could be inflicted by a rusty nail protruding from a dock, carries the risk of infection by tetanus. A booster dose of tetanus toxoid should be given every five years.

Poliomyelitis is much more common in other parts of the world than in the developed countries, and this is another vaccine normally given in infancy, with booster doses at intervals, which should not be neglected. Smallpox vaccination is now not necessary as smallpox has been virtually eradicated worldwide. Other vaccinations may be recommended for certain areas, depending on which countries one is cruising to, and local health offices will advise on this. In many countries there are regularly cases of enteric fever (typhoid and paratyphoid), so that the TAB vaccination is a sensible precaution for anyone sailing extensively abroad.

Malaria

There has been an upsurge of the malarial parasite worldwide and it is an increasing health problem affecting many pleasant cruising areas, such as the

Solomon Islands and Papua New Guinea. It is also endemic in many parts of central and southern America, Africa and South-East Asia. Malaria takes a particularly heavy toll on children and so prophylactic tablets should be taken all the time one cruises in a malarial area. Again local health offices will be able to give up-to-date information on which areas are affected.

The usual prophylactic drug is chloroquine taken weekly, the dosage being one eighth of the adult dose for infants under one year, one quarter for those one to four years old, one half for the four to eight year olds, three quarters for the eight to twelves, while those over twelve can take the adult dose. There is a chloroquine syrup available, which may be easier to give to small children than tablets. Some antimalarials such as pyrimethamine are not recommended for the under fives. Amodiaquine, which previously had been formulated for infants, has since been discovered to have the serious side effect of affecting white blood cells in some people, even leading to their death. Mefloquine is a new drug which may be more effective in choloroquine resistant areas. Initial testing on 100,000 patients in Thailand suggest mefloquine may be safe for children and pregnant women.

The upsurge in malaria is partly due to an increased resistance of the parasite to drugs such as chloroquine, and advice should be sought in a particular area about this resistance and which prophylactic drug is recommended. Up to date advice can be obtained from MASTA, a medical advisory service for travellers, run from the London School of Hygiene and Tropical Medicine, Keppel St, London WC1E 7HT. A fee is charged for this service.

There is a lot to be said for mosquito netting, against not only malarial mosquitos, but also other insects. These insects rarely fly far from the shore, so it is when anchored close by the shore or tied to a dock that they can present a problem. One of the worst places we were afflicted was in the enclosed sounds and rivers of North Carolina, while sailing along the Intracoastal waterway. Detachable frames with mosquito netting can be made to fit over hatches or alternatively netting can be rigged up over or across a child's bunk. Certainly it is a much better solution where babies and small children are concerned than smothering their sensitive skins with insect repellent. Prevention of the bite is also easier than trying to keep a small child from scratching an insect bite, with the attendant risk of infection.

Medical chest

A basic first aid kit should be mandatory on any boat and there are plenty of commercial kits on the market to choose from. For a longer cruise a more comprehensive selection of medicines than those contained in most kits will be necessary in order to deal with a wide range of possible illnesses and injuries away

51

from professional help.

The following is a recommended list for an offshore cruise, in respect of children; it does not include drugs for adults. Those items marked with an asterisk are only available on prescription in most countries. Some of the items will be discussed in more detail later in the chapter.

Cotton wool
Waterproof adhesive dressings in a variety of sizes
Sterilised gauze
Bandages and surgical tape
Crepe bandages for sprains
Sterile packs of dressings specially prepared for burns
Scissors, forceps, safety pins, thermometer
Disposable syringes and needles
Sterile needles with sutures for stitching a wound
General disinfectant (Dettol, pHisohex, Cetavlon)
Antiseptic cream or solution (Savlon, Cetavlex, T.C.P.)
Calomine lotion to soothe sunburn or insect bites
Promethazine cream for the prevention of infection in minor burns and insect
     bites (Phenergan)
Promethazine elixir as a sedative and hypnotic as well as for allergies to food,
     insect bites, jellyfish stings (Phenergan)
*Antibiotic cream or powder (achromycin or neomycin)
*Antibiotic tablets or paediatric suspension (ampicillin,amoxycillin)
Laxative
Antidiarrhoeal
Analgesic (painkiller such as paracetamol)
*Local anaesthetic for stitching or cleaning a major wound
*Ear and eye drops (framycetin)
Antifungal preparations for athlete's foot and other fungal infections
Piperazine sachets for threadworm and roundworm (Pripsen)
Shampoo for head lice (malathion or carbaryl)
Antiseasickness tablets
Antimalarial tablets or syrup (chloroquine)
Sun-screen cream

To this list add any special medicine that your child may need, such as for asthma or eczema.

As a general principle, the dosage of a medicine for a child can be calculated on his body weight as a proportion of an average adult weight. However, certain drugs used by adults are not recommended for small children, so attention should be paid to the manufacturer's accompanying instructions. Medicines in liquid or syrup form are much preferred by children and paediatric formulations should be bought for the medicine chest wherever possible.

With my pharmacist's training, I organised the medical locker on *Aventura* extremely carefully. Inside each bottle of tablets I put a note giving the name of the drug, its use and dosage, just in case the labels came off (which they never did) but also in case someone else apart from me had to play doctor. The bottles were packed in watertight boxes, in fact empty icecream containers of a hard plastic. All the non-urgent items were put at the back of the locker and the commonly used ones, such as antiseptic, near the front. Items that might be required urgently were also kept near the front, organised into different coloured plastic bags. One contained everything needed for burns, while another held all that was needed to treat a serious cut or wound. The disposable syringes and needles were carried because these are not available in many countries and hepatitis is a real risk from improperly sterilised needles. When we needed to be immunised against cholera after an outbreak in Tarawa in Kiribati (the Gilbert Islands), we took along our own needles and syringes.

Needless to say, if small children are on board, the medical locker should preferably be out of easy reach and also kept locked.

The potency of most medicines decreases with age and this is accelerated by the poor storage conditions that prevail on most boats and especially in humid tropical conditions. Potent drugs such as antibiotics should be renewed every couple of years, and drugs usually have an expiry date printed on the packaging. Drugs can be used after the expiry date if nothing else is available, but probably they will be less effective and the dosage may have to be increased. For those drugs for which a prescription is required, most family doctors are quite willing to oblige if the reasons are fully explained. Many doctors will also advise anyone setting off on an ocean passage which drugs are suitable for children's use.

Whenever a child is ill, it is advisable to try to obtain medical advice as soon as possible. The radio, whether VHF, marine or amateur, is usually the best way to achieve this, requesting *medico service*. Normally this will result in the caller being connected to the casualty department of the nearest hospital. Amateur radio is becoming increasingly popular on yachts and is ideal when cruising out of VHF range. Many of the amateur maritime networks based in various parts of the world, as for example Hawaii or California, have medical specialists on 24 hour call. The usual procedure is to describe the symptoms and what drugs are available in the boat's medicine chest. The doctor then can advise a suitable course of treatment over the radio. For urgent medical advice or assistance, the correct signal is MEDICO followed by PAN-PAN repeated three times.

Part of the problem when one is away from home base is to know when a symptom is serious enough to seek advice. The following list may provide a guideline for an anxious parent.

Symptoms for which medical advice should be sought

- Acute abdominal pain with vomiting
- Vomiting blood
- Head injury followed by vomiting, drowsiness or a fit
- A convulsion or fit of any kind
- Progressive drowsiness especially with a raised temperature
- A cough associated with rapid breathing and pain
- Headache at the back of the head
- Stiffness of the neck in a sick child
- Earache or suspected hearing difficulties
- Loss of weight

As well as common minor ailments which are not serious enough to seek outside help, situations may arise where medical advice is difficult to obtain or maybe a radio is not available. Some of these common complaints and their treatment will be examined in the following pages.

Seasickness

Small babies rarely appear to suffer from seasickness and this condition usually only appears after the age of six months. A lot of children who have grown up on boats are never afflicted, while a few suffer quite badly and others are seasick to varying degrees. Although the reasons why some people are more afflicted than others is not known, psychological factors can make seasickness worse – especially the behaviour of over-anxious parents.

When talking to long distance voyagers for a survey, I found that about half of the children suffered from seasickness to a greater or lesser degree, especially for the first few days after a lengthy stay in port. None of these parents gave any medication to their children, not even to children who suffered more severely. The usual remedy for seasick children was to encourage them to lie down in their bunks with a favourite toy or a good book. It is also important to keep the children from being bored or cold. Fortunately children to not have to deal with boathandling or watchkeeping, so it does not matter if they are lying down or drowsy a lot of the time.

An empty stomach sends a similar signal to the brain as the feeling of being sick, so it is important not to let the stomach get empty too often. One way to prevent this is to give a child small snacks at regular intervals between meals, such as a banana, some crackers or biscuits. This keeps a sense of fullness in the stomach.

Children have a marvellous natural resilience and often will adapt to adverse conditions more readily than an adult. Unlike adults they are less likely to feel ashamed or worried about the physical act of vomiting, especially if the parents make little fuss about it. In my experience it is most likely that ten minutes later they will be wanting something to eat. My own children were occasionally sick in heavy weather especially after a long stay in port, but I cannot ever remember them missing a meal.

It always surprised me what violent motion the children were able to sleep through, although their normal cabin was the fo'c'sle, which is the least comfortable part in rough weather. Often when it was rough they slept elsewhere, the cockpit cushions on the main cabin floor being the favourite place. It was better to have to step over a happy sleeping body than to have a miserable seasick child conveniently out of the way.

Many of the drugs which are most effective against seasickness, such as cinnarizine (Stugeron) or promethazine (Avomine), are not recommended for children under five. Those over five can take half of the adult dose. Children under five could take a quarter of a tablet of dimenhydrate (Dramamine), the six to twelve year old dose is half a tablet and the over twelves can take the adult dose. This drug is not recommended for infants under one year old. Personally I would hesitate before giving any drugs to a child for seasickness, only doing so if the child is in real distress about the condition, or maybe if an older teenage child is seasick.

Stomach upsets

Changes in the normal routine, different foods and drinks can all help to give an upset stomach, either diarrhoea or constipation, the latter being a common complaint on boats.

Many of the stronger antidiarrhoeal preparations are not recommended for children and cannot be bought without a prescription. An effective solution for a child is to give a large spoonful of a simple kaolin suspension, which any chemist will make up without a prescription. This will usually settle most minor diarrhoea. Children over five years can be given a kaolin mixture with added codeine.

If the diarrhoea is severe or continuous, it may be necessary to give something stronger, but it is very important to check the correct dosage and give only a drug that is recommended for children. For example, one tablet of Lomotil (diphenoxylate hydrochloride with atropine sulphate) can be given twice a day from one to three years old, three times a day for four to eight year olds, and four times a day for nine to twelve year olds. Older children can be given two tablets three times a day. Lomotil is also available in liquid form where one 5 ml spoonful is equivalent to a tablet. An alternative drug to use in cases of bacterial diarrhoea or gastro-enteritis is Ivax (neomycin sulphate in a kaolin suspension), where one to five year olds can be given 5 ml (one teaspoonful) four times daily and older children 15 ml (that is, three teaspoonfuls) four times daily. A prescription is needed for both of these drugs and they should be used with caution.

If one is cruising with a baby under one year old, one of the reasons for recommending breastfeeding for a more prolonged period than on dry land is that this does lessen the risk of diarrhoea in the baby.

One of the dangers in continuing diarrhoea is dehydration and the fluid intake of the child should be kept up. If a child has trouble in keeping fluid down, it is worth trying a thin purée of potatoes, which lines the stomach wall. An excellent replacement fluid if available is the fresh juice from the young green coconut. This has the right balance of essential salts and straight from the nut the added advantage of being sterile. Children do become dehydrated much more rapidly than adults, and so whenever diarrhoea or vomiting persists, for whatever reason, the child should be encouraged to sip sweetened water.

The opposite problem of constipation is often met with while cruising, sometimes because of changed diet or reduced consumption of fresh fruit and vegetables. Older children who start sailing for the first time may feel inhibited about using the head or making a smell or noise when in the confines of a small boat. Reassurance and a no-fuss attitude by the parents should help to overcome this.

The first solution to the problem of constipation is to increase the child's intake of water, fruit and bran cereals. Try and encourage the child to go to the head as soon as he feels the urge, not to ignore Nature's call, as some children are prone to do if they are absorbed in a game or lying in their bunks. A mild laxative, such as syrup of figs, can be given to help the emptying of the bowel, but should be stopped as soon as possible. Laxatives can be harmful as they may irritate the bowel and can help constipation to turn into a chronic problem as well as starting the habit of relying on a drug. They should only be given if there is pain or bleeding associated with really hard stools.

Bed-wetting is another problem that may distress a child or cause him to be concerned about a weekend sailing trip. A surprising number of healthy children take several years to achieve full control over their bladders and this applies more to boys than girls. Mainly it is due to a delay in the maturation of the relevant part of the central nervous system. Psychological factors can make it worse, for example if the child is insecure or worried about finding his way to the head in the dark or while the boat is in motion.

It is unreasonable to blame a child for something he does in his sleep, so the most important treatment is to reassure the child and reduce his feelings of anxiety about it. Punishment of any kind, even verbal admonition, is likely to do harm and delay control. Cutting out drinks for a couple of hours before bedtime and making sure the child empties his bladder before turning in can help. Also a dim light can be left on, if apprehension about getting up in the dark appears to be one of the causes. Over the years scores of drugs have been tried for this common childhood problem, but with little agreement among the medical profession as to their success. If bed-wetting persists in children over five, the most successful treatment appears to be a special pad, which the child wears and which activates an electric buzzer to wake him as soon as the first few drops of urine touch the pad.

Sunburn and heat illness

The effect of the sun is stronger at sea, partly because the air may be less polluted which, combined with the reflective property of water, intensifies ultra-violet rays. Also one may often be less aware of the sun's strength due to wind and breezes blowing over the skin. For these reasons the amount of exposure to sun that a child is getting should be carefully monitored until a protective tan has developed. Very blond and red haired children tend to burn much more easily and may need a protective sun-filter cream, although this should be applied warily to sensitive skins, checking that no allergy develops. Covering the child with long sleeved cotton clothing such as loose pyjamas may be a better solution, while babies and infants particularly should always wear a sun hat. A few children never develop enough tan to protect their skin and will always have to be protected from the sun in some way or another; but, for the majority, once a healthy tan is established they need take few further precautions. If sunburn does occur, it is treated as any other burn and in severe cases an antihistamine cream such as promethazine (Phenergan) can be used to prevent infection.

When sailing one moves much more slowly into a new environment compared to many other methods of travel, and so a certain adaptation to a hotter climate takes place gradually. Heat illness, either as heat exhaustion or a heatstroke, can occur, although this is most likely to affect those who are unacclimatised, as when flying in to charter or visit friends. In certain areas where the temperature is extremely high, for example in the Red Sea, heat illness is a risk for all members of the crew.

The symptoms are a listlessness accompanied by headache and nausea. The pulse is usually rapid and the skin feels clammy. Sometimes a prickly heat rash can develop. These symptoms can progress to a heatstroke, when sweating stops, leaving the skin dry and burning. Collapse into unconsciousness can occur in this case, but the most dramatic effect is the sudden rise in body temperature.

The most urgent action is to cool the child and reduce the body temperature. Strip the child naked, put him in the coolest place and sponge with cold water, iced if possible. Directing a small fan onto the skin will also help. The next priority is to replace the fluid and salt loss, by drinking water or lemonade to which salt has been added in the proportion of one teaspoon to one pint (5 ml to half a litre). As this is not very palatable, it should be taken in small sips to prevent vomiting.

In very hot climates a good preventive measure is to drink more than usual and increase one's salt intake by adding more salt to meals or by taking salt tablets. Meals should be light when eaten in the middle of the day, and exposure to the midday sun reduced. If a child does become listless, it is wise to step up his salt and water intake immediately.

Skin infections

Nearly every long distance cruising family I have come across in tropical climates has had at one time or another trouble with infected cuts or insect bites, which can turn into tropical ulcers at alarming speed in some areas. Eventually I learnt to painstakingly disinfect and treat every minute scratch, graze or insect bite, that normally we would not have worried about.

At the first sign of any infection the cut should be treated with an antibiotic cream or powder containing neomycin or tetracycline, or alternatively a sulphonamide powder. Powders can be more effective than creams under the moist tropical conditions that bacteria thrive in, because the cut is kept drier. I found that all treatments became less effective as the years we spent sailing in the tropics increased, presumably because we were lowering our resistance, which was only solved by a return to a temperate climate. Neomycin aerosol sprays can cause the side effect of deafness if used on damaged skin on any part of the body and are not recommended in the treatment of infected cuts.

These recurring infections are usually due to a staphylococcus infection, a common affliction among those cruising in the tropics, and this has to be treated by an internal course of an antibiotic to eliminate the bacteria from the bloodstream. The importance of treating all minor cuts and grazes seriously while sailing in warm climates cannot be emphasised too strongly.

Not only bacteria, but other organisms also, love damp conditions and fungal infections such as athlete's foot are much more common afloat than ashore. As children are so often barefoot and in wet conditions, the feet stay damp and are therefore prone to catch this condition of cracked broken skin that itches and can become very red and raw. Drying the feet well and keeping them exposed to air helps prevent the infection, sandals being preferable to socks and shoes. Dusting the infected area with a powder such as zinc undecenoate (Tineafax) or tolfanate (Tineaderm) is effective.

Nits and worms

Children seem to have a talent for picking up certain things that adults rarely do, such as threadworms or head lice, especially when they are travelling. The first sign of the latter is usually the nits or eggs that stick to individual hairs and an infestation of this sort is easily cured in a few days by shampooing with a specific shampoo containing carbaryl or malathion.

Threadworms can be equally effectively dispatched with piperazine, usually sold as a raspberry flavoured powder which is made up into a drink. Dosage is according to age: one third of a sachet from three months to one year old, two thirds of a sachet for the one to six year olds, while over six a whole sachet can be given. Threadworms are not serious and only annoying because of the itching around the anus at night. If children never ate with their fingers or put their fingers in their mouths without first washing them, then the infection would be eliminated. Unfortunately few small children can be relied on not to do this. If the infection does recur, it might be worth dosing the whole crew.

Swimmer's ear and ear infections

When children are in and out of the water continually, especially if they dive or go underwater a lot, they are very susceptible to ear infections. One way to prevent this is to make sure they dry their ears effectively with cotton wool when they come out of the water. There is also a drying solution containing glycerol which aids drying and a drop is added to each ear after swimming.

If at all possible, medical advice should be sought in all cases of ear infection or earache. This is to check that the ear drum is not perforated, because there is a risk of permanent damage and deafness if some antibiotic ear drops, such as framycetin, are used when the ear drum is perforated. Infections of the external ear can be cured by these drops, but for otitis of the middle ear an internally administered antibiotic may be necessary. Some of the antibiotic ear drops are also formulated as eye drops, so they can be used in bacterial infections of the eye, styes and conjunctivitis.

Serious infections

Nearly all serious infections are likely to require antibiotic treatment and these are drugs which must not be used indiscriminately or treated lightly. Medical advice should be sought either ashore locally or over the radio as to their use and dosage for a child. However, if one does not have a long range radio, or one is in a remote area or on an ocean passage, it may be essential to begin treatment quickly and a decision will have to be taken on a course of treatment.

If an ocean passage is to be included in the cruising plans, it is worthwhile discussing with one's doctor which drugs would be most suitable for a child, especially as a prescription will be required. Many antibiotics are available as syrups or paediatric suspensions, which are easier to give a child than a tablet. It is also a good idea to stock more than one antibiotic in the medicine chest, as different antibiotics are effective against different ranges of bacteria. Some people have a sensitivity to penicillin and if possible try to discover whether this is the case beforehand.

Ampicillin is one penicillin derivative which is effective against a wide range of infections and can be bought both as a syrup and a powder which makes up into a solution, especially formulated for children. The powder is in a sealed bottle and, when required for use, distilled water is added and the bottle shaken. If distilled water is not available, ordinary water should be boiled and left to cool before making up the solution. Some other antibiotics which are available in suspensions suitable for children are amoxycillin, effective in respiratory, genito-urinary tract and ear, nose and throat infections, and Septrin (trimethoprim and sulphamethoxazole) which can be used by those sensitive to penicillin. Tetracycline is an antibiotic in common use, which is effective against a wide spectrum of bacteria, but it should *never* be used for children under twelve years of age. The full course of an antibiotic should always be followed, even after symptoms have subsided, and any solution left over should be discarded as it does not keep once it is made up.

Treatment with antibiotics can be quite dramatic in its success, as one example might illustrate. Sailing in the Caribbean, we spent several days anchored off Saline island, an uninhabited island north of Grenada and close to Carriacou. One evening my daughter Doina, then nine years old, felt slightly unwell and was running a temperature. I wondered if she might have a slight intoxication from fish, as freshly caught fish figured largely in our diet. The next morning, however, her temperature had risen alarmingly to 40°C (104°C) and I began to get worried. There seemed no real reason for her high temperature nor any other symptoms, but on inspection her throat and tonsils did look slightly red and swollen. Immediately I started giving her a course of ampicillin and also a rub down with cold water. The response to the antibiotic was quick and in 24 hours she was back to normal, although I did continue the treatment for another two days to be sure the infection was controlled.

An attack of appendicitis is something that many parents fear and is one of the most likely reasons for acute abdominal pain in children and young people. Antibiotics can suppress appendicitis until port is reached, although an operation may still be necessary. This is one good reason for carrying antibiotics in the medical chest while cruising. In fact, if a child complains of abdominal pain, it might well be only a stomach upset due to something eaten or because of constipation or diarrhoea, but it does no harm to check for appendicitis. The following symptoms provide a guideline.

(1) A vague central pain, which settles into a sharp pain in the lower right abdomen. There will be tenderness in this area when touched.
(2) The child usually vomits once or twice after the pain begins.
(3) Maybe there is one loose evacuation of the bowels at first, but then constipation sets in.
(4) A rising temperature and a steadily rising pulse rate occur. A rising pulse rate, which can go up every hour, is the surest sign that treatment is urgent.

If appendicitis is suspected, firstly give no solid food of any kind at all, just sips of plain water to relieve thirst. Secondly, begin a course of ampicillin or penicillin. Do *not* give a laxative for the constipation as any irritation to the intestines can increase the chance of the appendix rupturing. Make the child comfortable, propped up in his bunk; heat applied to the painful area with a covered hot water bottle can relieve the pain. An analgesic can be given (suitable painkillers for children are discussed in the next section).

The pulse should be taken every two hours and the temperature every six hours. The first sign that recovery is taking place is that the pulse rate begins to slow back down to normal. A child's pulse rate is usually higher than an adult's, especially babies and infants, being about ten beats a minute less when the child is asleep. (As the range of normal pulse rates is large, it might be worthwhile noting a child's normal pulse rate while in good health.) Other signs of recovery are a decrease in the pain, the temperature returning to normal and the cessation of any vomiting. Nevertheless appendicitis can easily flare up again, so the child should be kept on a light diet and resting until port is reached and a doctor can be consulted.

Treating a child's pain

If a child is in pain, from a bad wound, fracture, serious injury or for some other reason such as appendicitis, he cannot be given the same painkillers as adults. Most strong analgesics are not recommended for children, mainly because an overdose can have serious consequences. A suitable analgesic for children would be an elixir of paracetamol. Although not recommended for those under three months, babies over that age and up to one year can be given a 5 ml dose (one teaspoonful) four times a day. One to five year olds can take 10 ml (two teaspoonfuls) four times a day and the over fives the adult dose of up to 20 ml (four teaspoonfuls) four times a day. Paracetamol is also an antipyretic and so will act to bring down the temperature of a sick child as well.

For very severe pain as might result from a major accident pentazocine could be used, either in the form of capsules or as an injection. Over one year of age, the dose of the injection is calculated on the body weight of the child. The capsules are only recommended for over six year olds and all these pentazocine preparations need a prescription. They should never be used if there is a head injury.

A better solution for a sick child than giving painkillers is to give a sedative, such as promethazine (Phenergan elixir). This can be given to small children from six months old and also has a hypnotic action which will help a sick child to sleep. This elixir is very useful to have on board as it also has an antihistaminic action against allergies and can be used if a child gets an allergic reaction to food, insect bites or jellyfish stings.

A healthy diet

Ensuring a balanced and healthy diet will increase a child's chances both of successfully resisting infection and of combating disease or injury should it occur. It is not too difficult to keep a good supply of fresh food on a boat if items are properly stored. Fruits such as apples, oranges and grapefruits store well, either

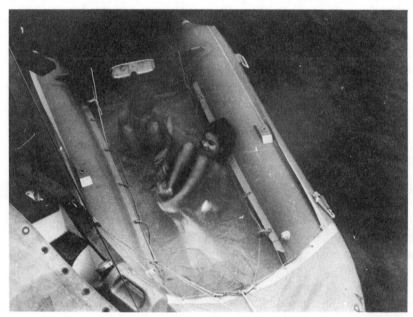

After a torrential downpour in Panama, Ivan and Doina enjoy a bath in the water collected in the dinghy.

individually wrapped in newspaper or suspended in net bags. Potatoes, onions, carrots and hard salad cabbages are some vegetables that can be stored for a considerable time, the two latter being of higher nutritional value if eaten raw. The secret is in the shopping, and all fruits and vegetables should be hand picked and chosen for their quality prior to a passage. A stem of bananas hanging in the rigging is a trademark of boats sailing in the tropics and the fruits can be picked off the stem as they ripen. Carefully selected green tomatoes slowly ripened on our passage across the Atlantic, lasting almost to the final day. At no time in our circumnavigation were we completely without some fresh produce, even if it was sometimes unusual, such as green pumpkin tips or unripe green papaya, which can be grated and mixed with a salad dressing.

A growing child does need plenty of protein and often in places where fresh meat is difficult to find fresh fish can be caught or bought instead. Smoked and processed cheeses are another source of protein that have a long storage life and the dried pulses, such as beans, peas and lentils, should not be ignored. If eggs are fresh they usually keep for six weeks without any further treatment.

The easiest course of action if one is in any doubt about diet while cruising is to take a daily supplement of multivitamins, a procedure that can do no harm. As the body does not store some of these vitamins, it is more important to have a daily intake of a smaller quantity than a larger amount all at once, a principle which also applies to fresh fruit.

In interviewing over a hundred long distance voyagers at various times in the Pacific, some twenty-five of whom had children with them, and from my own experiences during a six year long circumnavigation, I have drawn the conclusion that children on boats are a distinctly healthy lot. I have not come across any cases of appendicitis nor any of the childhood infections such as measles or mumps. The only serious medical problems reported to me were two cases of viral infections of unknown origin, one of which resulted in severe dehydration of the small child and necessitated a speedy transfer to a local hospital. In general, children seemed more resistant than adults and the constantly changing atmosphere that cruising brings had helped them build up a healthy resistance to many diseases and infections.

Books

The Ship Captain's Medical Guide. (1967) London: HMSO.
The Essentials of First Aid. (1983) London: The Order of St John.
Counter, R.T. (1985) *The Yachtsman's Doctor.* London: Nautical Books.
Eastman, P. (1974) *Advanced First Aid Afloat.* Cambridge, Maryland: Cornell Maritime Press, Inc.

6
Babies and Infants

A gently rocking boat is an ideal cradle for a sleeping baby and the very young are usually quite content in a watery environment. Until their mobility and desire to be entertained increases, small babies create few problems if they are kept fed, clean and secure. Without the conveniences of a modern home, achieving this requires a certain amount of organisation, but fortunately there are many products on the market designed for travelling with small children, whether by land, sea or air, which help make life easier for the parent of today.

First and foremost in requirements is a snug and secure place for the baby, which he cannot fall out of in a seaway. As berths on a boat are normally adult size, this is best achieved by putting a small baby to sleep in a basket or carrycot, usually with handles on it so it can also be used for transporting the child. The cot must be wedged firmly into the bunk so it cannot slide about, which can be done easily with cushions or pillows. If the weather is rough, the baby himself might need to be stopped from rolling in some way, such as with a folded-up blanket or towel tucked along his side. If a basket or carrycot is not used, the baby must be wedged firmly in the bunk so that there is no danger of suffocation should he roll to one side. Only at about five to six months old will a baby be able to roll over from his front onto his back or vice versa on his own.

There are various types of travelling and folding cots on the market, even some that convert to baby seats or adapt into a pushchair as well. The choice will depend on how much space is available and whether the cot or basket has to serve elsewhere apart from on the boat. A cot of plastic material has many advantages in a salty atmosphere; it is easier to keep clean and will not become damp as some natural fibres do in moist conditions. The natural fibres of a basket, however,

64

Brigitte Sperka and Frances Stocks on board *Aventura* in Bali. Both their six month old daughters already had hundreds of miles of sailing behind them.

are much pleasanter to the touch than plastic. A softer basket may be easier to store out of the way when not in use, yet a cot with rigid sides can be wedged more easily into a bunk, the sides of the cot providing extra protection for the baby.

The bunk should have a leeboard or leecloth high enough to contain whatever the baby is sleeping in. Netting can be fixed from the board or cloth to completely enclose the bunk, so that in no circumstances will the baby fall out. This netting should be fastened with hooks or studs so that it can be opened easily when required.

A carrycot is a bulky item to store on a boat, and once a baby can sit and crawl a basket or cot can be discarded if space is at a premium. Even so, all small children must be tucked into snug berths that they cannot easily fall out of and sandwiched with cushions or pillows to stop them moving about too much. Equally one must be sure that nothing can fall onto them from nearby shelves or other berths. One solution is a high leecloth that can be clipped up at night and let down in the day. This cloth should be reinforced and strengthened so it will stand up to the daily wear and tear that is normal with an active child. An alternative to a leecloth is a wooden board which can be slotted in at the edge of a bunk, but a permanent arrangement of built-in higher sides to a child's bunk might be worth considering. This is only possible if the berth is not also used as a day settee. If the children have a separate cabin or the forepeak berths this can be arranged more easily. On our boat the wooden sides to the children's berths in the forward cabin were built much higher at the head end of their bunks, although these sides tapered away towards the foot.

Out of the way

Netting which encloses the entire bunk and can be fastened up to the ceiling from the outside can be used with older active infants too, not just to keep them safe while asleep, but also while they are playing. This playpen arrangement not only stops the child getting out, but at the same time allows him to see what is happening in the rest of the boat, where his parents are and what they are doing.

Most of the points made in the earlier chapter on safety afloat apply particularly to babies and infants. A crawler or toddler on a boat requires almost constant supervision and can rarely be left to his own devices without some watch being kept over him. It is not only that toddlers can hurt themselves or fall overboard, but they can also easily cause trouble by twiddling the dials or moving settings on radios, autopilots or Satnavs. It is difficult for a small child to understand that these things are not to be touched, especially instruments that have digital readouts blinking so attractively. Keeping radio contact with the Canadian yacht *Kleena Kleene II* as we sailed at the same time across the Indian Ocean and up the Red Sea, Bill Stocks was late for our schedule several times because his one year old daughter had detuned the radio. In an emergency such a mishap could be crucial.

Some method of keeping an infant out of the way has to be considered, such as a netted-over bunk, which can only be opened from the outside by an adult. In an emergency situation, when both parents may be needed on deck, a way of quickly immobilising a small child safely must be found. While a netted-over bunk is one solution, another is to strap the child into a seat similar to those used in cars and from which he cannot undo himself. A car seat itself could easily be adapted to fit over a settee berth, being firmly attached to anchoring points as in a car. These seats are easily removed when required, leaving only the anchoring points and webbing attached.

In such circumstances, give the child some of his favourite toys and, if he still objects, ignore him and get on quickly with the task in hand. A few minutes' crying will not do a small child any harm – not as much as leaving him unrestrained and unwatched, or neglecting a vital job in the sailing of the boat. As children grow up, they will soon come to realise that in certain situations the handling of the boat takes precedence over anything else and that parents are best not bothered in these circumstances. The safety of the boat must always come first.

Feeding baby

The old adage that mother's milk is best is nowhere truer than on a boat, and in fact most sailing mothers I have met have carried on breastfeeding their babies much longer than they probably would have done living on land. This does avoid the need for sterilising bottles and the extra storage space required for the equipment involved in bottle feeding. However, a few mothers choose to bottle feed so that the father can also be involved in feeding the baby, especially sharing the night feeds, and this does have a certain advantage, particularly on an ocean passage. If a baby is being bottle fed, the bottles and teats can be sterilised by leaving them in a sterilising solution in a container with a tight fitting lid, proper sealing of this unit being vitally important on a moving boat. As infant formula has to be made up with boiled water to avoid infection, it is more convenient to make up a whole day's supply at once, but this can only be done if there is a refrigerator on the boat to store the bottles in, or alternatively an insulated container with ice or frozen icebags. Infant formula should never be kept warm for any length of time in a thermos flask or stored in warm conditions, because this encourages the growth of bacteria. All feeding equipment should be sterilised until babies are at least four months old. In warm climates the formula will have to be made up as required if one has no refrigeration, keeping the opened packet in as cool a place as possible.

Apart from the performance of sterilising bottles and making up formula, one reason sailing mothers breastfeed longer, often even after their babies are old enough to drink from a cup, is that breastfeeding greatly reduces the risk of stomach upsets and diarrhoea, particularly important when cruising away from home in foreign waters. In some developing countries infant formula is not available except on prescription, a measure which has been introduced to encourage women to breastfeed in these countries and so reduce infant mortality and illness due to inadequate sterilisation of infant formula mix.

Fresh milk is rarely available in the tropics, although the advent of UHT (long life) milk has greatly improved matters for sailing families. Although closer to the real thing than powdered milk, UHT milk does not quite have the same taste as fresh milk, and cold fresh milk was one of my children's delights when we arrived in countries like New Zealand and Australia. Carrying powdered milk in the ship's stores does not save weight because one has to carry the extra water needed to make it up. The cartons of UHT milk are thus one way of conserving fresh water supplies and an important standby if water is in short supply or is polluted. Fruit juices are now also available treated in this way to increase their storage life.

Breastfeeding can be very tiring, especially in the early weeks when more night feeds are given, and this tiredness can reduce the flow of milk. If possible a nursing mother should not have to do night watches at all. Many parents avoid longer passages until their baby sleeps through the night or else take on extra crew for the passage. After the birth of their son Tristan in Suva, Ian and Derry Hancock took someone with them to help sail their 30 foot *Runestaff* on the passage from Fiji to New Zealand, although they did not normally take on crew. Any delay in their departure would have meant staying on into the hurricane season in the South Pacific, which they were loathe to do with a small baby. Six week old Tristan sailed this 1,000 mile ocean passage without any problems at all.

For weaning a child, proprietary infant foods and cereals are now available in all major ports worldwide, but in remoter places the selection may be more limited or non-existent. However, many parents do prefer to give their child as much fresh food as possible and not rely on these convenience foods. Infant foods can easily be made from the fresh food of an adult meal, selecting small quantities of everything and grinding or sieving these to a mush suitable to be spooned to a baby. There are several small hand blenders or grinders on the market that achieve this, usually by rotation of the handle which turns grinding blades on a sieve. In most places, fresh fruit and vegetables are available even if it is only the ubiquitous banana, which is one of the easiest fruits to mash up for a baby. With milk and sugar it is a favourite of most small children. If in doubt about the adequacy of a diet for a child while cruising and the amount of fresh food available, extra vitamins can always be given. Spoonfuls of orange juice or rose hip syrup will provide vitamin C, and cod liver oil vitamins A and D. Even those parents who normally insist that their growing baby eats only fresh food can still be glad of being able to quickly open a tin or jar if the weather is bad or sailing conditions are tough. Babies rarely suffer from seasickness, but that does not mean that parents are also exempt, and so a quick solution to feeding baby is the answer in bad weather.

The other end!

The disposable nappy has made an enormous difference to cruising with a baby. For a weekend or short cruise disposables are the obvious choice, with one proviso: that one is careful where one disposes of them. Although marked as disposable and bio-degradable, the haphazard discarding of these items has polluted fringing reef and beaches in some places. Out at sea is fine, but one must be careful when near a beach or the shore. Collecting them into a tightly closed sealed bag and disposing of them ashore on one's return might be better.

Disposables are great for a weekend sail, but parents on a longer cruise often choose to use the terry towelling sort as well. Disposables are not always available in remote places and stocking up for a long period poses a problem as they are very bulky items to store. The amount needed for one small baby for several months would fill a whole bunk. They can also work out an expensive item for parents on a limited budget, especially if bought in countries where they are imported and not manufactured locally.

Many mothers cruising for longer periods of time use disposables for passages and terry cloth while in port where washing facilities and fresh water are more readily available. A limited water supply and the lack of a washing machine does make washing nappies an unwelcome chore on a sailing boat. However, it is not insurmountable, particularly if a sterilising powder (such as Napisan) is used. This powder is dissolved in cold water in a bucket with a lid; the nappies are then soaked in this solution overnight and only need to be rinsed out the following morning in fresh water. The thorough washing and rinsing is important in order to remove all the ammonia which results from the breakdown of urine. This is an irritant and easily causes a rash on a baby's sensitive skin. Frequent changing and careful drying of the baby's bottom can minimise the likelihood of a rash. In hot moist climates plastic pants will promote the formation of ammonia and also increase the chance of a heat rash, and so are best not used.

Water

Washing the nappies is just one of the ways that fresh water is consumed at an alarming rate when a baby is on board. As baby skin is sensitive, washing both skin and clothes in fresh water is necessary to prevent salt water sores or rashes. The amount of fresh water needed with a baby or infant on board is something that must be taken into consideration when planning for a cruise. If the water storage capacity of a boat is limited, extra fresh water can always be carried in jerrycans lashed on deck. Special black thermal bags which are left out in the sun filled with water are an easy way of having a supply of hot water without electricity.

A large plastic bowl can act as a baby bath and double up for washing clothes, but this is yet one more bulky item to find storage space for. There are some space saving baths available, such as an inflatable bath, or a plastic sheet bath, where a heavy plastic sheet is suspended on a frame which can be unclipped and folded away. On *Aventura* we installed a large domestic size stainless steel sink in the galley, as all sinks made for boats appeared to us to be extremely small, whether for washing dishes or a child.

Some ingenuity may be needed to control the amount of water used, but a baby does not get very dirty at sea and it is not necessary to bath a baby every day. Face, hands and bottom can be kept clean without using a lot of water and, if fresh water is very limited, a sponge down is a perfectly adequate alternative. The washing water can be used easily for something else such as soaking the nappies.

Transferring young children safely on, off or between boats requires care and attention, preferably with both hands free.

Thinking of dual purposes for items can also help to reduce the amount of gear carried, for it is all too easy to be buried under mounds of baby chairs, cots, baths, pushchairs, toys, etc. It is worth considering very seriously if some of these items can be dispensed with while living on board.

Transporting baby

The most hazardous moments when cruising with a small baby are getting on and off the boat, especially from a dinghy while at anchor. There is little room on most boats for prams or pushchairs, even the folding stroller variety, so methods of carrying the child about the body are popular with boating parents.

The slings and carriers for babies either carry the child in front of the body or on the back. For the tiny baby, the soft sling that holds the baby close to the chest is probably the most convenient. The baby feels content near to the parental heartbeat and it is easier for the parent to see how the child is. These fabric slings are like a pouch; some have a neck support for the newborn and others have a protective outer cover which zips around the carrier seat. An older child who is heavier may be more tiring to carry in front and, if the baby can already keep his back straight in a sitting position and does not need his head supported, a backpack type of carrier may be more suitable. It is certainly easier to carry a heavy infant for longer periods in this way. On the back the baby is more exposed and one cannot keep an eye on what he is doing, but it does give an older baby a better view of the world. Some of these backpacks with rigid frames can also be used as a baby seat, which can justify the extra space they take compared to the foldable fabric slings.

The advantage of all these types of carrier is that they leave both the parents' hands free for getting on or off the boat, carrying shopping or whatever. With baby in front, all one has to be careful of is not to bump the child as one climbs aboard, but as the child is close and visible this is not difficult to avoid. When leaning forward it is safer to cradle the baby's head with one hand.

Some parents feel that the baby is more protected if transported in his basket or carrycot, but this is a two handed operation and not so easy to attempt on one's own. When handing a child up and down in this way from dinghy to boat, it is essential that one has a firm stable footing. The dinghy should be attached both fore and aft securely with short painters and one must be careful not to push the dinghy away from the boat as one hands up the baby and cot. In this operation there will only be one hand free to steady oneself against the side of the boat.

Babies do not have the same capacity for temperature regulation as adults and so are more susceptible to the extremes of the weather. Also they have no way of communicating if they are too hot or too cold apart from crying. Care must be taken to protect small children from too much cold, especially wind or spray when transporting them over water. The sun should be treated with equal caution, for tender young skins and eyes are particularly vulnerable and direct exposure to strong sunlight should be as brief as possible for babies. Some exposure is unavoidable when going to and fro, although a cotton sun hat with a brim to shade the eyes is easily worn. As fresh air is so beneficial one does not want to keep a baby inside the boat all the time, so a canopy or tent should be rigged up over the cockpit when the sun is strong. A large cockpit tent is essential for cruising in sunny climes and even while sailing some protection for a child can be easily rigged up with a smaller piece of canvas.

Frances Stocks of *Kleena Kleene II* particularly recommends the use of a sheepskin for a baby to sleep on. By trapping air, it provides insulation when it is cold and helps the baby's skin to keep cool when the weather is hot. Frances found it invaluable, as her daughter Brandi would sleep anywhere in the boat and under any conditions as long as she was on her sheepskin. A sheepskin does not need to be washed as often as one would imagine.

Amusing a small child

A deterrent to many parents contemplating making a passage or spending a longer time cruising must be the prospect of amusing a small child at sea. Small babies are no problem, as rocked by the wave motion they are probably happier than on shore. Eyecatching mobiles strung up in their line of vision will amuse them as the mobiles move with the movement of the boat.

A small chair into which an infant can be securely strapped is also useful, not only for feeding the baby, but so that he can see what is going on inside the boat instead of lying gazing at the ceiling. Similar to a seat for immobilising a toddler, an infant's chair must be firmly secured or anchored in some way, so that the lurch of a wave does not tip the baby out or the chair over. Some chairs have a small tray which can be fixed in front of the child to hold toys or a plate when a baby starts to feed himself. Due to the increase in travel by all means, not only on the water, there are various portable high chairs or adaptable seats on the market. One simple portable chair clamps onto any solid table, yet folds away quite small when not in use. This type of chair is only suitable for a child who can already sit unaided, and unless the child can be securely strapped in he should not be left in such a chair unattended.

The same toys that amuse a small child ashore will amuse him afloat as well, and although children do differ in their tastes, most acquire one favourite cuddly soft toy which should never be left behind. There is normally plenty of activity and movement on a boat to catch the attention of an infant and until a baby becomes mobile there are few problems in amusing him. Once a child can crawl or walk the difficulties begin and some children find it very restricting to spend a lot of time in the confines of a boat instead of running, jumping and being active as they would be on shore. Children vary enormously in character, some being more active than others, but generally smaller children have less capacity to amuse themselves than older children. They may well demand the attention of an adult to read a story, sing nursery rhymes or play games with them.

The British couple Sylvia and Ian French considered that amusing their son John took most of their spare time, especially on passage, during the three years they spent circumnavigating in their 27 foot sloop *Pomona*. Along with keeping watches and the general work involved in running a boat, amusing John meant that they had little time left to do other things. They had planned their world cruise while John was small so as to be back home in time for him to commence school at five. Later, on reflection, they considered this was not so important as they had originally thought and that sailing with him at an older age might have been more rewarding.

Similarly, the task of occupying their two daughters under five was one of the main reasons why Vicki and John Holmes of *Korong II* returned home to Australia to live ashore after a two year cruise in the Pacific. Several years earlier,

Playing with young Kevin takes a lot of Françoise Pitteloud's time, especially at sea.

before they had children, they had undertaken another extensive cruise and so noticed the difference that children made. Attentiveness to the young girls' safety and keeping them amused left little time for the parents to enjoy themselves how they would have liked to. Although 43 foot *Korong II* was a spacious well-equipped boat, fitted out with young children in mind and even with a washing machine on board, Vicki Holmes still found life afloat with a couple of under-fives very exhausting. The Holmes' grumble that they could rarely go out of an evening was echoed by Max Fletcher of *Christopher Robin*, who also complained that babysitters were not easy to come by when living afloat.

Although there are special problems in sailing with the very young, a little thought and organisation can easily surmount them, much depending on the attitude of mind of the parents. In the survey of long distance voyagers we carried out in the Pacific, out of the twenty children on fourteen boats, ten were under the age of five and four of these had been born since the start of their parents' voyage. These children had all grown up knowing little else except the sailing life and were well adapted to life on a boat. As they knew nothing else, they regarded life on a boat as normal and nothing special at all. Perhaps cruising with infants was best summed up by Max Fletcher of *Christopher Robin*, whose son Christopher was only nine months old when the Fletchers set sail from Maine

73

on the east coast of the United States in their Westsail 32. When I spoke to him in New Zealand, Max told me, 'Cruising with a young child was so much easier than I thought it was going to be.'

7
Making the Most of a Holiday Cruise

As an increasing number of parents take their children to sea, there comes a point when something a little more exciting than a day trip beckons across the horizon. Even the most dedicated racing enthusiast may decide to change his style for a family holiday. While some families may be content to potter around the shores of their home area, others may prefer to take a cruise that is a little more adventurous, and there are few children who do not enjoy the excitement of going to foreign places. From the south and east coast of England, France, Holland or Belgium are but a day's sail away, while Mexico beckons to the Californian and down-east from New England leads to Canada.

Another possibility for making a change from the home cruising area is to take a charter holiday, which also may be one way to decide if the family really likes cruising before investing in a suitable boat. The number and diversity of bareboat charter companies has risen dramatically in recent years, offering the attractions of cruising in beautiful faraway places without the expense and time involved in taking one's own boat there. Flotilla sailing among the Greek islands and bareboat chartering in the Caribbean are the two most popular cruising holidays, although charter operations are to be found almost anywhere the cruising is good, from Tahiti to Tonga, Yugoslavia to the Great Barrier Reef in Australia.

The more exotic is, of course, the more expensive and some parents may have doubts about whether it is worthwhile to spend such money on a family holiday.

Nevertheless sailing in an area where the weather is sunnier and more predictable is a great attraction for those living in colder climes. Children may learn to enjoy sailing much more readily when the air is warm, the sea temperature perfect for swimming and when any spray that comes on board is warm spray. Whatever kind of cruising one does, whether one splashes out on a charter holiday or is content to enjoy the known pleasures of home waters, it is still worth making some effort to ensure that a child both enjoys himself and gains from the experience.

Jobs for children

The first step in fostering a child's interest in sailing is to involve him as much as possible in the sailing of the boat. This not only keeps the child busy and occupied, but also gives a sense of achievement and pride in mastering the skills involved. One way of increasing a child's sense of participation is to designate a particular job as that child's sole responsibility.

Even quite young children can be found jobs to do, such as scrubbing the decks or tidying and coiling ropes. When they were small, my children enjoyed making a round cheese of the sheets on the aft deck, particularly winding the large main sheet very carefully. With all the ropes neatly coiled or decoratively wound, it meant our boat looked shipshape too. Putting on the sail covers and lacing them up when one arrives in port is another job that fairly young children can manage to do successfully, and two small ones can help each other if the cover is too bulky for one to manage alone. Learning to tie proper knots is something that most children enjoy, from putting a simple figure of eight in the end of a sheet to the more complicated bowline on a mooring line. Once one is satisfied with their knot tying skills, children can get on with tasks such as tying on fenders, while even those not trusted with knots can easily take the fenders off and pack them away tidily.

Early in our cruising life, my son Ivan was designated the flag officer, with the responsibility of raising and lowering our ensign, courtesy and code flags, and folding them away neatly. He took this job very seriously, especially after we acquired a complete set of code flags, learning all the letters, codes and how to dress the ship overall in the correct fashion. Identifying the flags of other countries became one of his hobbies, although the skipper of a small motor boat in Sicily, flying the Panamanian flag of convenience to avoid local taxes, did not appreciate being told by a six year old that he was flying it upside down. Ivan kept a flag folder as part of his school work, drawing and colouring each new flag he spotted, making a note of where and on what vessel he had seen it. He also found out about the origins of some of the flags which often reflect the history of the country concerned.

An older child of seven or eight can handle the jib sheet if the wind is not too strong or alternatively can tail for an adult pulling in the sheet. Selftailing winches are an aid as far as children are concerned because they can be operated with two hands. Sometimes my two children would pull together on the sheet so as to gain the necessary muscle power. Handling the jib sheet when the sail is hoisted, or adjusting it when the point of sailing is changed, is one job that a child can do without going on deck but from safely inside the cockpit and still feel a sense of participation in the sailing of the boat.

A small sail such as the mizzen or a staysail can be given over entirely to a child as his responsibility. If the sail area is not too large or if it is a sail used only in lighter airs, the child can feel the satisfaction of hauling it up and setting it correctly, maybe even learning to decide when it should go up or come down, depending on the point of sailing or weather conditions. After a few years of sailing, I made a mizzen staysail to help push our heavily laden boat along a little faster in lighter breezes. Doina and Ivan took this sail over completely as their sail and were in charge of hoisting it, although as it was a three handed operation they did employ the skipper on one of the sheets. To set a large sail correctly needs more strength than most children are likely to possess, but if they are enthusiastic to try, let them hoist as much as they can before an adult tightens those last few inches.

From around ten or twelve years old, children can be a positive help on a boat, no longer mere passengers but able to share in the work load. That means that if one parent is off watch and snoozing in the daytime, he or she need not be wakened if a sail needs changing, a bonus on a longer passage. By the time children are teenagers they should be capable of being full members of the crew, tackling nearly all the tasks of handling sails and boatwork that an adult would.

Nearly all children love to take the helm and even the youngest can have a closely supervised turn, although he may need some extra lift in the way of cushions so that he can see where he is going. If there are points of interest, such as buoys to round or a shoreline to follow, the child's attention can often be held for longer periods before he gets tired or bored. There is a lot of satisfaction to be had by children at the wheel or tiller, for it does make them feel that they are in charge and that the boat is under their control.

On many cruising boats the helm will be taken over by the automatic pilot or selfsteering gear, but an equal feeling of being in charge can be obtained by the child standing a watch. Among the many families I have met cruising, almost all the children over the age of ten or eleven took full daytime watches. Sometimes two younger children stood a watch together, while older teenagers also stood a night watch, often the first one of the evening. Children usually respond very well to being given responsibility and take the jobs they are given very seriously. Start by giving a child a short watch of maybe half an hour and keep an unobtrusive eye on how attentive the child is being, checking that he is not too easily distracted into playing games or reading. It is helpful if the circumstances when the watchkeeper should alert the skipper are explained carefully, such as another vessel approaching, sighting land or a buoy, or the appearance of a threatening black cloud.

Navigation is another subject in which it is easy to arouse the interest of children and which they usually enjoy because it enables them to follow the progress of a cruise more closely. Even those children who do not enjoy sailing all that much can be quite keen to find out how soon the destination will be reached. Most children are fascinated by charts and pore over them, picking out landmarks they have recognised, or puzzle over identifying a certain rock, island or other feature. Checking the number on a buoy with binoculars or timing a light with a stopwatch can be fun, not a chore. Quite early on, my children learnt how to use the handbearing compass and with a little help could transfer their readings into lines on the chart to pinpoint our position. Ivan became so interested that he mastered using the sextant, too, and by the age of ten could take a reasonably accurate noon sight and work out our position. A cheaper plastic sextant that we had as a back up was given over to him, so he could take sights in parallel with his father and compare results.

Some of the tasks the children undertook were not strictly necessary but just an interesting diversion. A favourite was to estimate the speed of the boat by one child dropping a piece of paper off the bow and the other child timing its arrival at the stern with the stopwatch. From the time taken for the paper to travel the length of the boat, the speed can be calculated. If the paper takes x seconds to travel the length of the boat (y), it would travel $60/x \times y$ feet in 1 minute. Multiplying this figure by 60 gives the distance travelled in 1 hour. For example, if the paper took 5 seconds to travel the length of a 35 foot boat, it would travel $60/x \times 35 \times 60$ feet in 1 hour. To find the speed in knots, the distance travelled is divided by the number of feet in a nautical mile (6,080) For the example quoted above this works at 4.14 knots.

If instruments such as depth sounders are down below at the navigation station, children can be useful messengers in relaying data such as the depth to the skipper on deck, who maybe is carefully looking out for dangers when coming in to anchor, or so he knows how much anchor chain to let out. Our standard method of coming into an unknown lagoon in areas of coral reef or coral heads was for Jimmy to climb the mast while I remained at the wheel, unfortunately out of hearing because of our wheelhouse. This was solved by stationing one of the children on the aft deck to relay the skipper's commands, 'ten degrees to port', 'ten degrees to starboard', or 'keep straight ahead'.

It is not only the fun side of sailing that children can take part in: they should also help with the less popular tasks too. That inevitably means the washing of the dishes, which appears to be the least popular chore on a boat as well as on shore. Our two children took it in turns to wash up, one taking odd dates and

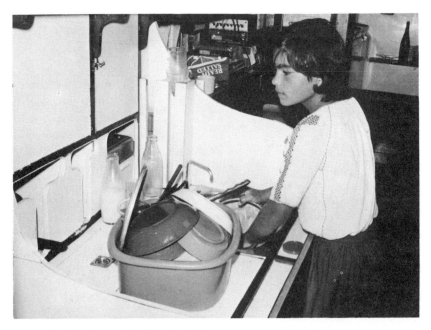

Washing the dishes is one job children can do.

the other evens, with Jimmy solving the problem of 31 day months by doing that day himself. Many children enjoy cooking, but this is one job that has to be handled very carefully when at sea because of the danger of scalding. Yet even that can be solved in some way or another, such as an enthusiastic young cook making a cake, which the adult supervises putting in and taking out of the oven. For younger children it might be wiser to restrict their culinary activities to when one is in port or at anchor.

Involving the children fully in all aspects of life on board is an excellent way of counteracting any boredom that might result from being confined in a restricted space at sea. The lack of space is most noticeable where active children are concerned and never so much of a problem with the kind of child who is happy curled up in a corner with a good book, whether he is at home or at sea. Children vary enormously in temperament and character, so that there can be no hard rules; an activity which is perfect for one child can be a pain for another. Certainly if one's child is happy reading on his bunk or listening to his favourite music tapes, there is no merit in forcing him into spending a lot of time on deck.

While at sea the opportunities for an active child are more limited; in port or at anchor there are plenty of activities where a child can expend excess energy, from swimming to rowing the dinghy. The challenge of climbing the mast is regarded as a great sport by many sailing children and we have motored into several anchorages in calm weather with two children perched on our spreaders.

Doina spinnaker flying in Tonga, a sport that most cruising children enjoy.

Like little monkeys, children swing from ropes and sheets or play in the rigging and ratlines, especially on larger, older boats with heavier gear. Even on a smaller boat, the bosun's chair shackled onto the mainsail halyard can make a swing that will keep a child occupied for quite a while.

Another marvellous pastime is that of spinnaker flying, but warm water is essential for this or else a hardy constitution. The anchoring arrangement of the boat has to be changed so that it is anchored or moored from the stern, with the stern into the wind. A bosun's chair or similar canvas seat is then suspended between the two tacks of the spinnaker or cruising chute. Climbing into the seat in the water and stretching apart the tacks with the hands, the person is lifted up to fly above the water as the wind fills the sail. How high one flies depends on the strength of the wind and one's weight, although the spinnaker halyard can be payed out to increase this height a little. In fact, a light breeze which will not lift a grown man out of the water is ideal for children, whereas the stronger winds needed to give a man a good ride can lift a child frighteningly high. A line attached to one tack and left slack can be used to bring down a child who has had enough – or more likely one who refuses to give anyone else a chance.

Diaries and logbooks

After participating in sailing the boat, one of the most rewarding things a child can do is to keep a diary or logbook of his cruise. A special book can be bought and its cover decorated with illustrations, photographs or designs, with the title of the cruise in bold letters. Books with both lined and unlined pages are ideal so there is space for both drawings and descriptions. Alternatively a file can be used so that the number of pages can be easily added to and different kinds of paper utilised. A smaller child might use a book that has half a page plain for drawing with a few lines underneath on which he can write about his drawing. As well as drawings, the diary can be illustrated with postcards of places visited ashore, or entrance tickets to museums, even bus tickets. An older child who takes his own photographs could use these to illustrate his diary. For the little ones not yet able to write, the same idea can be followed in a scrapbook with big coloured plain pages. They can be helped to paste in postcards, tickets and any other bits and pieces they may have collected while on trips ashore. Cutting out the pictures from tourist brochures is another colourful source for illustrating a scrapbook.

There are many variations in what can go into such a book, depending on a child's age and interests, from drawing and identifying marine life to the history of places visited. Sometimes my children's diaries were more of a catalogue of what they ate or the games they had devised for their own amusement than the sights they had seen, but those were things that were important for them. A particular harbour might be remembered for the fact that it had a shop on the quay selling delicious icecream rather than for the old castle guarding the harbour entrance.

Some older children may prefer to keep their logbooks more in the style of a ship's log, in which they can note the distance travelled, wind speed and weather conditions, lighthouses or buoys passed, or the names of other vessels seen at sea. If the cruise area is rich in history, as many of the European coastlines or the New England coastline of America are, the diary or scrapbook can help to keep the historical sites visited fresh in the children's memory. Cruising guides which give some of this history or other books about the places visited are useful to have on board to stimulate an interest in the area being cruised in. (More ideas about subjects that could be included in the diary or logbook can be found in chapter 16.)

Not only does a child get more out of cruising by keeping such a diary, but it also remains as a treasured momento, something to show to friends when one returns home. My children have kept diaries in various places and always got great enjoyment and much hilarity out of rereading them at a later date.

Hobbies and interests

Cruising also offers an ideal opportunity for extending a child's special interest or hobby, as well as introducing new pastimes which a child may not have thought of before or had the opportunity to pursue. Starry nights in the cockpit with the pair of binoculars that almost all boats possess could well stimulate an interest in astronomy or at least in identifying stars, planets and constellations. A good map of the night sky or a star finder is essential and the easiest way to learn the constellations is to identify one or two of the well known groups, such as Orion or the Great Bear, and then work out other constellations from their position in relation to these. Few navigators nowadays use the stars, and with the advent of satellite navigation probably even less will in the future, but the subject may still catch the imagination of a child intrigued by how the sailors of yesteryear found their way across the oceans without the instruments of today.

As mentioned earlier, spotting flags of different countries or code flags is another hobby that some children might like to follow. We also had a little book, *I-Spy at Sea*, which gave points for different kinds of ships, buoys, lighthouses and other features that could be spied at sea. If there is more than one child on board, these spotting games can be run as a friendly competition. Another idea for this kind of observation game is to collect unusual boat names.

Children are often avid collectors and those who already collect stamps, matchbox labels or who press wild flowers will find plenty of opportunities to collect other items too. Beachcombing among the flotsam and jetsam yields all kinds of unlikely items, from glass fishing floats to wood or glass eroded into peculiar shapes by the action of wave and water, as well as a wide variety of natural objects from seaweed and egg cases to shells and pretty pebbles.

Shell collecting

One of the most popular hobbies among sailing children is collecting shells, whether scavenged from beaches or collected by swimming underwater. To increase a child's interest it is worth buying a book on shells, so the child can try to identify the specimens he collects or at least classify them into their families. Background information on various shells will also help to make the collection more interesting. The true collector will keep a record not only of the name of the shell, but where it was found, the type of habitat and depth of water.

The shells found on the seashore and even many of those in the sea will be dead and empty, but some collected by diving or in rockpools will still have the owner inside. Cleaning these living shells can be quite a problem. The simplest method is to gently heat the shells in fresh water, then prise the dead animal out with a pin, bent wire or other suitable utensil, such as one uses for eating shellfish or snails. Unfortunately this method cannot be used on the porcelain type shells such as cowries or olives, because heating them makes the shiny glaze go cloudy or crack and so ruins their beauty. For these shells there is no simple solution. I usually waited for them to die by leaving them out of water, then tried to remove as much as possible of the dead animal with a jet of water and various implements. Then I suspended them from the side of the boat in a mesh string bag. Gradually little fish and other small creatures devoured the remains. The whole operation can be quite odiferous and a poor sense of smell is a great advantage.

This problem of cleaning shells was one of the reasons why we did not take too many of a particular species, although the more attractive shells did make appreciated presents for friends. The main reason, though, is so as not to denude an area, but to leave plenty of shells to create the following generations. For a similar reason any stones or slabs that have been turned over to look for shells should be turned back again, because minute eggs and other small creatures may be on the underside and will perish if exposed. Shell collecting has become so popular that unfortunately whole areas have been virtually stripped clean by commercially minded people who have only their own profit in view and not any conservation of the species. Therefore it is very important to teach children not to take more than they need. This is sometimes difficult when a pretty variety is in apparent abundance. In a lagoon in the Society Islands, Doina and Ivan discovered they could track down the long pointed auger shells by following their trail through the sand to where they had buried themselves. The children became so fascinated by the success of their detective work and their free diving prowess, that in the end I had to call a halt to their collection of this species.

The only shells that can be harmful are a few species of the cone family, which release a small dart to kill their prey. This dart contains a poisonous substance which has been known to be fatal, particularly from the white and brown blotched *conus geographicus*. It is prudent to take hold of all cone shells from the back, keeping the aperture pointing away, and then any dart is released away from the body. The majority of cone shells are harmless and the cone family is one of the most popular among collectors, as it has such a striking variety of colours, pattern and shapes. It is also prudent never to walk barefoot on a reef and to look very carefully before touching anything or turning over stones, keeping fingers out of open clam shells. A small stick can easily be used instead for turning over stones or prodding into gloomy corners.

Dolphin watching

There can be few cruising children who do not welcome the company of dolphins and enjoy watching these beautiful animals riding the bow wave or disporting themselves beside the boat. Some children may be interested in taking this diversion a little more seriously by acting as observers for organisations which are interested in sightings of dolphins and whales. These organisations, usually university research groups, provide forms on which to record the information they require, and they also have available guides to the identification of cetaceans, which is the family name for dolphins and whales. There are a surprisingly large number of species, the common dolphin being only one of some twenty-five species which have been sighted in the North Atlantic area alone.

The most important features to record are the estimated size of the animals, the shape of the head and snout, the size, shape and position of the dorsal fin and, in the case of whales, the size and shape of blow. Identifying the exact species is not easy, especially in rougher weather, and even experienced observers can have difficulty, so it is far better to record simply 'dolphin species' along with the description of as many features as can be seen, including body colour and markings. Other information which is important is the exact location of the sighting (latitude and longitude), the date and GMT time, the number of animals in a group and the presence of any young animals, their direction of travel and behaviour, such as jumping or bowriding, as well as any seabirds associated with them. Details of weather conditions, such as wind direction, force, state of the sea, wave height and visibility, are also important. Even reporting areas of the ocean where no dolphins or whales were seen is of value to scientists evaluating all the data they receive.

Further information can be obtained from:

Dolphin Survey Project

Report Form

Send to : Mr D.A. McBrearty, M.A.,
Dolphin Survey Project,
Dept. of Anatomy,
University of Cambridge,
Downing Street,
Cambridge, CB2 3DY.

Name of Observer: ....

Vessel: ....

Address: ....

....

Behaviour/Activity pattern of dolphin: Feeding, playing,
bowriding, leaping; shape of school pattern. How close
are the animals and do they show any interest in your
vessel?

Is a photograph/slide/film available ....

INTERNATIONAL DOLPHIN WATCH

Date: .... Time: .... GMT .... Local.

Ships position Lat .... Long ....

Weather Conditions: .... Sea Temp ....

Number seen: Adults .... Juveniles ....

Estimate of length .... Juveniles ....

Species ....

Observed characteristics from which identification is
made. eg. colour pattern, shape of dorsal fin, flipper
shape, type of beak (long, short or absent).

Please try to make a sketch of the animal you see.

Peter Evans, UK Cetacean Group, Edward Grey Institute, South Parks Road, Oxford, OX1 3PS, England.

Denis McBrearty, International Dolphin Watch, Department of Anatomy, Downing Street, Cambridge, CB2 3DY England.

James Mead, Division of Mammals, Smithsonian Institution, National Museum of Natural History, Washington, DC 20560, USA.

Steve Katona, College of the Atlantic, Bar Harbor, Maine, USA.

Steve Leatherwood, Hubbs Sea World Research Institute, 1700 South Shore Road, San Diego, CA 92109, USA

William Perrin, National Fisheries Service, Southwest Fisheries Center, La Jolla, CA 92058 USA.

Apart from shell collecting or dolphin spotting, many children may like to take a more serious interest in any marine life encountered, whether it is identifying a fish caught at the end of the line or seabirds skimming over the waves. Useful additions to the shipboard bookshelf are small reference books on seabirds, fish and other marine life, both that found along the seashore as well as on the high seas. It is amazing how much there is to observe if one does keep one's eyes open – not only seabirds or fish, but brightly coloured sea snakes wriggling along, turtles lazily basking on the surface or the gauzy blue butterfly wings of the by-the-wind-sailor. The keen young naturalist might like to keep a notebook with detailed descriptions and drawings of the wildlife he observes, much in the style of the dolphin sightings.

Fishing

Fishing is an ideal occupation to pursue while afloat, whether the child hangs hook and line over the side while at anchor or trawls behind the boat while sailing. The latter method can result in some quite large catches when the assistance of an adult may well be required. Small children need careful supervision when using fish hooks because when these become embedded in fingers or hands they can necessitate a hospital visit for their removal. An alternative for the younger enthusiast is to attach a net to a long stick, which can also be used in shallow waters along a beach or for retrieving lost objects. Underwater fishing with a spear gun is better left to older teenagers who can be trusted to operate this equipment safely.

All the forms of fishing, from rod and line to nets or spearguns, do provide great satisfaction for children, especially when the catch is suitable and large enough to be eaten. Similarly providing the family dinner by collecting mussels, cockles or other shellfish can be an occasion of pride.

Sports

Many older teenage children who sail become proficient fishermen both above and under the water. Snorkelling and diving are also popular pastimes among these children. Diving with air tanks does require proper training and should never be attempted by an untrained person. If a young person does become interested in sub-aqua diving, there are many clubs and organisations where professional training can be received. However, even a beginner who is just learning to swim can don mask, snorkel and flippers and so discover the beauty of underwater scenery, even if only looking down from the surface. All of this equipment can now be bought in small sizes, and snorkelling might provide just the incentive needed for a youngster to improve his capability in the water. Many of the children I have met who have been cruising in warmer waters for any length of time have been very able free divers, spending as much time exploring under the water as swimming on the surface.

All the water related sports are easily pursued from a boat and many charter companies provide not only scuba gear of flippers, masks and snorkels for their clients but also equip their boats with sailboards. Recently the sport of sailboarding has greatly expanded and many boats now find space on their decks to store a sailboard. Many of the latest boards are not easily handled by a younger person and a certain strength is required of a child before he can pull the

A tender which can be rigged for sailing gives children a lot of pleasure.

sail and wishbone up out of the water, although there are some junior boards on the market. A small sailing dinghy might be more easily managed by the younger members of the crew and has the advantage that more than one child can enjoy themselves in it at the same time, instead of waiting for turns. Finding space to stow a sailing dinghy is one of the biggest problems on all but the largest boats, although some of the smaller sized dinghies such as the Optimist will fit on the foredeck or coachroof and can double as a tender. Some inflatable dinghies can also be rigged to sail and this might be an attractive alternative for family cruising.

Children do get great pleasure out of messing about in the dinghy, whether they sail or row, especially when this gives them the chance to do some exploring on their own of inlets and other corners of a harbour. Obviously one should be satisfied that the children are capable rowers or can handle the sails before letting them venture too far afield. While a dinghy that can be rigged for sailing or one that rows well is a boon while cruising with children, it then becomes almost essential to have a second dinghy, even if only the smallest inflatable. Otherwise one is likely to find oneself marooned on a boat at anchor when the children have disappeared both out of sight and out of hearing, which I know from experience can be extremely frustrating.

In this chapter I have tried to outline some of the ways that children can enjoy themselves while on a cruise, helping to sail the boat, keeping a logbook or diary and pursuing various hobbies or sports. By making the most of their holiday or short cruise they will be well on the way to becoming enthusiastic sailors with enduring memories of their experiences.

8
On Passage

Making a longer passage has to be considered as soon as one thinks about cruising further afield. Even if not absolutely necessary, it is often the quickest way to get to one's destination instead of hopping along the coast and stopping every night. Especially if time is limited, many families might consider a longer passage at the beginning or end of their holiday to allow more days in their chosen cruising area. The idea of a longer passage may well cause cruising parents to hesitate as they wonder how they are going to amuse their offspring out of sight of land. The two problems that immediately come to mind are boredom and the confinement of an active child to the restricted space of a boat. Children who are normally very energetic and do a lot of swimming, other sports or just running about, may find being cooped up on a small boat for several days or even longer rather frustrating. Providing an outlet for their energy is not easy, and there is no quick solution to this problem. The key lies in keeping them fully occupied and involved in other things, so that the other problem of boredom has less time to rear its head.

If the weather is fairly benign children can be quite active, not only inside the boat but also out in the cockpit or on deck, harnessed if necessary. When the weather deteriorates even the most lively child usually slows down and many children are content to spend more time in their bunks, especially if they have any feelings of seasickness. Involving the children in as much of the sailing of the boat as possible not only gives an outlet for their energies but also gives them the feeling of being needed and useful. Many of the ways in which children can help on a boat were outlined in the previous chapter, from washing up and cooking

The locks of the Panama Canal provide an interesting diversion after a long passage.

to handling smaller sails, jib sheets and giving a helping hand, such as by finding a shackle key, passing a winch handle or sail ties. Children over the age of ten usually take at least a short daytime watch on most boats, which is a considerable help for a shorthanded crew. The length of time a child spends on watch, or if an evening or night watch is also stood, depends on the maturity and age of the child. Generally it is only children from about fourteen upwards who stand watches in the hours of darkness.

For children who are on a more lengthy cruise there will be schoolwork to be done, which occupies some of the day, the number of hours depending on the age of the child. On many cruising boats the children prefer to do more schoolwork on passage, not only to counteract boredom but to earn themselves time off when they reach port. On the other hand a few children do very little schoolwork at sea – mainly those who suffer from seasickness to some degree. A certain amount of flexibility has to be shown on passage, taking into account the particular child, even if the correspondence course followed requires work to be returned by a set date. Several of the parents who teach their children themselves vary the school routine at sea and include more oral work and reading, and less written tasks. In this way Doina and Ivan learnt their multiplication tables on passage as well as such items as French verbs and spellings. We kept longer writing projects for in port and never attempted chemistry experiments or anything of that nature at sea.

Special projects

There are many special projects that can be carried out on a passage, whether as part of the school routine or as a way of adding interest to the passage for children who do not have to do schoolwork. A typical project is to take daily weather recordings, which is something my children did on our Atlantic crossing. At the same time each day, the wind speed and direction can be measured, either by reading the electronic instruments on board, or by a small handheld wind speed indicator, which also incorporates a compass. The air and sea temperatures can also be measured; for the latter, the adult should fetch up a bucket of seawater into the cockpit, so the child can take the water temperature in safety. The temperature of the sea is especially interesting if one is sailing into an area of changing temperature, as when crossing the Gulf Stream. Other points which can be noted are the type of clouds and the appearance of the sky, the estimated height of waves and their appearance and the presence or absence of foam on their tops. If there are not suitable instruments on board, a child might like to devise his own method of measurement, such as making a rudimentary wind vane attached to a compass, or a simple rainfall gauge.

The results can be plotted in various forms, from a simple line graph with a cross showing the particular value recorded for each day to more complicated variations. Block graphs appeal more to children as the different items can be blocked in with different colours. A child can amuse himself in deciding how to make his weather chart, maybe giving different colours to different winds or, as Doina did, using little arrows to show wind direction. At the end of the passage an older child could construct a pie chart (a circle with segments corresponding to proportions) to show the percentage of winds encountered from different quarters. This type of weather recording appeals more to an older child, although a younger child can easily make a simple weather chart by drawing and colouring a symbol for each day – a yellow sun, clouds, rain or lots of wind – or alternatively cutting out symbols from coloured paper. However complicated or simple the chart is, it still serves as a permanent record of the passage for the child to keep. Watching the temperature rise or the number of yellow suns on the chart increase as one sails towards warmer places gives an incentive to everyone in the crew, not only the children.

Older children might also like to learn to navigate, to use a sextant and work out the boat's position. A second plastic sextant is a useful acquisition, both as a backup and for a child to learn with. Even if the navigator now uses satellite navigation methods, a child can still plot his own course alongside, challenged to see how accurate he can get. Using his navigation results and reading distances covered off the log, the child could mark in a track of the passage on a chart or a copy of a chart, even drawing in little symbols for events that occurred, such as strong winds, a thunderstorm or dolphins bowriding.

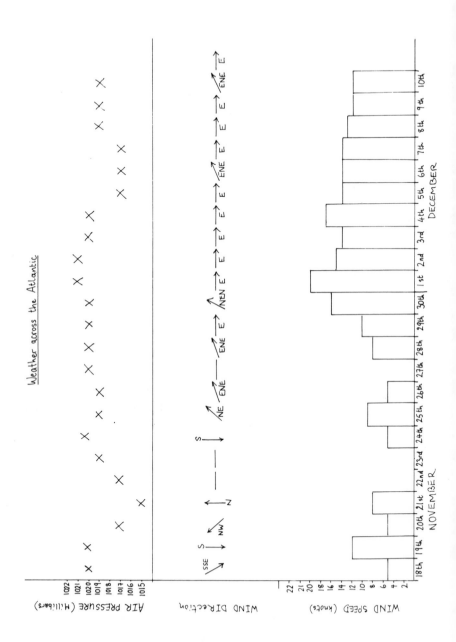

An example of a weather chart.

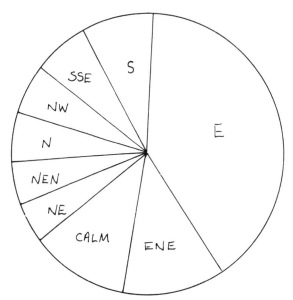

Pie chart to show direction and proportions of winds on a passage.

The young ones

Many of these projects are obviously more suitable for older children and not applicable to those not yet able to read or write. Such small children will also not be capable of taking part in any of the boatwork and watchkeeping and the onus of entertaining them lies heavily with the adults. Having more than one child does ease the problem, especially if they are close enough in age to play together. Sometimes it is not even playing, as Nina and Juan Ribas of *Abuelo III* explained when I asked how three year old Luisa occupied her time on passage. 'Mainly bothering her one year old brother,' was the reply.

Some aspects of amusing the very young were discussed in the chapter on babies and infants and a certain amount of time will have to be spent by parents reading stories and playing games with the children. This can be tiring when sailing shorthanded, but fortunately younger children do also usually sleep longer on passage. Space should be found for as many toys and games as possible, and particularly for the child's favourite soft toys. If a child is surrounded by his familiar toys from at home, not only does he feel more secure but there is no reason why he should not play and occupy himself as he would ashore.

Reading

Once a child has learnt to read and can enjoy a good book, life for the parents often becomes much easier. When I asked parents taking part in the ocean cruising surveys how their children amused themselves on passage, the most frequent answer given was reading. Only one teenager read very little, but occupied herself playing video games, a sign of the changing times maybe. The consumption of a book a day was not uncommon, being specifically mentioned by several parents. My daughter Doina was in this category and reaped the benefit of six years without television, as by the end of our cruise, at fourteen years old, she had become an extremely well-read young lady. The biggest problem with these avid readers is keeping up a suitable supply of reading material without lowering the waterline too drastically. This was usually solved by cruising children themselves and 'Have you got any books to trade?' was a familiar opening gambit for making friends on arriving in a new port. As children grow up they can also begin to dip into the adult bookshelf.

Books about the passage, or about other sailors who have sailed the same way in the past, can sometimes tempt a child who does not normally read much. These are interesting books to have on board even for readers who need little tempting, as are books about the place one is sailing to, of which more is said in chapter 16. Popular books with sailing children are those that involve the sea, such as *Two Years Before the Mast* by R.H. Dana or *Round the Horn Before the Mast* by Basil Lubbock, both contemporary accounts of life aboard sailing ships in the last century. *The Kon Tiki Expedition* by Thor Heyerdahl, Joshua Slocum's *Sailing Alone Around the World* and the various accounts of unusual voyages by Captain Villiers are all sea classics which, although not written specifically for children, are not too difficult for a young reader. Some voyages have been retold for younger readers, such as the excellent retelling of Darwin's voyage and work, published by Oxford University Press. In the fiction field, mention must be made of those perennial favourites among sailing children, the *Swallows and Amazons* series by Arthur Ransome, all thick enough to keep a child quiet and absorbed for a reasonable length of time.

Other activities on passage mentioned by cruising parents in the survey were looking at picture books by young non-readers, drawing, colouring and building things with construction toys such as Lego or Meccano. Making models was another pastime that absorbed some children and there is a vast range of kits on the market, from the very simple to the large and complex, so that something suitable can be found for almost any age of child.

Paper and pencil

A large supply of paper, drawing and colouring books, pencils, crayons and felt pens will never go amiss on a passage, and fortunately these items weigh little and do not take up much space. The possibilities with pencil and paper are almost infinite, from the simple pleasure of drawing from one's own imagination to the traditional noughts and crosses or various word games. There are books for children containing puzzles of all kinds from joining dots to crosswords and anagrams. Older children might like the challenge of making up their own crosswords – not as easy as it appears.

A pad of Altair designs will also occupy a child for a considerable time as he picks out the patterns from these complicated printed designs in different colours. Pattern making toys such as Spirograph can also fill time and, like all of the above pursuits, have the advantage that they do not need another person to play with. Similarly, paper folding in the Japanese style of *origami* fascinates many children and will keep those who are interested busy for great lengths of time. Paints can be a messy item on a boat and, except for boxes of block water colours, are best avoided. With the range of felt tipped pens, coloured pencils and other suitable painting sticks available, there is plenty of choice for artistic expression without making too much mess.

There are many games where little else is required except for pencil and paper, such as seeing how many smaller words can be made from one long word chosen at random. For example, 'navigation' can produce van, tan, tang, vang, vain, gain, ingot, nation, tango, etc. Younger children can be given the advantage of being able to use two letter words such as at, it, on and an, while an adult can be penalised by being restricted to only four letter words and upwards. The winner is the person who scores the greatest number of words.

Pinpointing a letter and then writing down a number of predetermined categories beginning with that letter is another universal word game. Categories could include boys' names, girls' names, towns, countries, animals, vegetables, birds and so on.

Another perennial pencil and paper game is that of joining the dots to make squares. A square of dots is drawn and then each player takes it in turn to join two dots together by a line. When a line completes a square the player may put his initial in it and then has the bonus of another go, which towards the end of the game can result in a whole chain of squares being completed by one player. The art of the game is not to draw a line which gives squares to your opponent, and the winner is the player with the most squares completed.

Games that need no equipment

If the motion of the boat is too much for drawing, painting or word games on paper, there are a lot of games that can be played orally, although these do require more than one participant. Many of the kind of games that people play on long journeys by road or train are equally useful on a boat and can be played sitting in the cockpit, or involving the participation of the person at the helm or

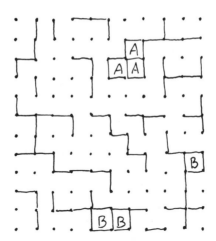

on watch, a useful ploy when the other parent is asleep below. The old favourite I-spy is a little difficult when there is not much else but ocean all around to spy, but there are alternatives. Even the I-spy game can be adapted into a competition to be the first to sight land, a lighthouse or buoy when nearing the end of a voyage.

Baiting a person by firing questions at him which he may not answer with either the words 'yes' or 'no' is popular with all ages, as an unwary adult can be trapped into 'yes' or 'no' without thinking, just as quickly as a child.

Another suggestion is alphabet games, where the players have to think of a town, animal or whatever one chooses for each letter of the alphabet in turn, a player dropping out when he fails to name something. Alternatively each player has to think of something starting with the last letter of the previously mentioned item; again different categories can be used, whether place names, girls' names, flowers or rivers. This can also be played with syllables instead of letters, for example – sailing – ingot – otter – terminal – and so on until a player cannot think of a word. Words already used may not be repeated.

Another simple word game is for each player to add a letter to the previous player's letter, but never to finish a word:

b
bu
bul   (but, bun, bug, would make the player lose)
bulw (bulb, bull, bulk would be losers)

The player must always have a word in mind, which he must give if challenged – in this case, 'bulwark'.

Another word game much enjoyed by most children is memorising a list to which each player adds another item when it is his turn to recite the list. This usually goes something like: 'When my Aunt Dolly went to Peru she took with her a hot water bottle, a pair of purple pyjamas, a mosquito net, a striped umbrella . . .' etc.

Board games

Board games such as Scrabble, chess or draughts (checkers), can also pass the time if one has a suitable opponent. Many of these games can be bought in a magnetised variety meant for travelling, very useful at sea where pieces can slide about all too easily. Trivial Pursuit is another currently popular game with many different general knowledge questions to answer. In fact, the cards of this game which have the questions on could be used on their own as a quiz without the board if there was no steady place to play it. My children also enjoyed backgammon, which has the advantage of being played at a faster rate than games like chess and so does not take so long to complete.

There is nothing to beat a pack of playing cards, for taking up the minimum of storage space and providing an almost endless variety of games. I am not going to give details of the many card games or patiences that can be played, as there are many books which do this so much better. Books on card games, word games and pencil and paper games might be worth adding to the boat bookshelf to provide ideas when inspiration fails.

Devising your own games

In many ways I consider that having long periods of time to fill, without the aid of external stimuli or the readymade entertainment of television, gives a great impetus to children to devise their own games and entertainments. This necessity to fall back on their own resources can have a constructive outcome and is one of the ways in which cruising can help develop a child's character. Constantly arranging something for the child to do may not always be the best solution, because there is much to be said for a child learning how to occupy himself. There is a real danger in today's world of having our leisure interests packaged and predigested for us, which, along with the bombardment of daily life by radio, television, magazines and advertising, can lead to a loss of the ability to amuse ourselves. Sometimes it might be wiser to stand back and see what the children come up with on their own.

A large collection of battered soft toys of various descriptions from teddy bears to rabbits, horses and monkeys, inhabited our forecabin and gave much warm sustenance to my children. They became almost members of the crew,

Bowriding dolphins are always welcome companions at sea.

particularly one large bear called Yellow Teddy, who lost an eye, an ear and most of his stuffing during his circumnavigation. Doina and Ivan spent hours with these toys, involving them in a variety of imaginary events, writing little plays for them to act out, arranging marriages between them or birthday parties for them. It always seemed to be one or other of the toys' birthdays and a special treat had to be found. Yellow Teddy's birthday became more elaborate each year and involved us adults in present giving, cake making and once even a trip ashore to a restaurant to celebrate his birthday in style.

Some of the plays they devised, mock interviews with toys or the Toyland News, they recorded on a small portable cassette recorder, using different voices for the various toys. This cassette recorder provided hours of entertainment, especially when it came to recording sound effects, which involved a great deal of experimentation. Recording on tape instead of writing is another possibility for schoolwork that is particularly useful on a passage; a recorder can also, of course, be used for playing music or listening to some of the story cassettes especially produced for children.

Listening to tapes is an activity that many children do on passage. The small personal stereos with headphones are popular and a boon if the children's musical tastes are different to one's own, especially as many children do like hearing their favourite pieces over and over and over again! These personal stereos also have the advantage that they can be listened to while lying in one's bunk and so are of great value when the weather is rough or a child feels queasy. When I asked parents what their children did in bad weather, several parents specifically mentioned that their children listened to music or story tapes. The cassettes with stories recorded on them are appreciated by small children as yet unable to read, and even older, reading children still enjoy them, especially if the weather is not so good. It does release the parents from the task of reading stories so they can get on with other jobs.

Surprises and hidden treats

Tapes are just one of the things that parents buy when they know they are going to make a longer passage. Most parents I have spoken to make various special provisions, buying new toys, books or games. Very often these are put away and produced at intervals during the passage, particularly when boredom sets in. The pleasure of a new toy can create a welcome diversion, especially for smaller children. A longer passage can be marked off into stages, such as the halfway mark, when a celebration and present giving can take place. Small gifts of toys or sweets can be wrapped up and hidden away before the passage.

On our crossing of the Atlantic, which took twenty-six days, we had a little party as we crossed each 10° line, with presents for everyone in the family and a few special goodies to eat. The presents for the children were chosen as items which I thought would keep them occupied for a reasonable length of time – puzzles, colouring books or models to make. After recounting what we had done to a friend in America when we left Maine on the next leg of our voyage down to the Panama Canal and the Pacific, this friend produced a small sack filled with wrapped surprise presents for all of us, and so these parties became a regular feature of all our passages over a week in length. The anticipation of the hidden presents and a special meal also gave the children an added interest in navigation so that they paid close attention to the plotted line creeping across the chart.

The only child

One of the drawbacks to spending a longer time afloat is the lack of contact with other children, and for this reason many parents counsel others to take more than one child to sea if at all possible. Yet many parents sail with a single child quite happily, although invariably they have to devote more time to that child than when there are other children aboard. Especially if the child is young, parents must be prepared to spend a considerable amount of time on passage amusing the child by reading stories or playing games with him. For a shorthanded crew of

Doina and Ivan cool off during a long hot passage in the tropics.

two, also having to stand night watches and sail the boat, this can be quite tiring. Often father will deal with almost all the boathandling and leave mother to amuse the child, while another solution is to take on an extra crew for longer passages. Older children on their own often devise their own ways of dealing with this singularity. One eight year old lived in his own world, peopled with characters out of his imagination, while according to the parents of another child, who was twelve years old, their son had developed an amazing ability to amuse himself.

Taking it easy

It is on longer passages that the advantage of a separate cabin or area for the children comes into its own. Then their toys and games can be left undisturbed, without worrying about tidying up and without overflowing into the rest of the boat. A major tidy-up can easily be carried out when one reaches port. There are few children who are naturally tidy; the vast majority are definitely not, and there is no harm in letting them sleep in a bunk full of their favourite toys if that is what keeps them happy. Being able to shut the door and ignore it all is an easy solution.

Most parents are a little more indulgent on passage than in port, while still respecting the discipline necessary for safety on board. If the children forget to wash or do not get dressed for a few days, it does not matter very much. Taking life easy on a passage has much to recommend it. In practice many children sleep more at sea than they do ashore, and this does not apply only to babies and infants. One of the biggest problems of passage making in fact often occurs on arrival in port, when tired parents are looking forward to a rest and sparkling, thoroughly rested children are full of energy and rearing to go.

PART TWO
EDUCATION AFLOAT

9
Taking the Decision

One of the major concerns for parents planning a longer cruise is the education of their children. It is a subject that may well discourage some parents who might otherwise be able to take some time off from their jobs, a sabbatical leave or be able to support themselves financially while cruising. The idea that they are unqualified to teach their children may frighten them into thinking they cannot possibly tackle the task. Yet parents teaching their own children is nothing new and was considered normal in the past before the widespread development of schools. It is quite usual in isolated rural communities, for delicate or sick children, or families posted to jobs abroad. Down the centuries adults have been imparting information and teaching skills to the next generation, very often by the child working alongside the adult, son beside father, apprentice beside master. That only those who have spent several years studying how to teach are qualified to do so, is a comparatively recent attitude.

One of the first requirements for being a good teacher is one that most parents will already possess – that is, having the child's best interests at heart: loving the child, caring about his upbringing, and wanting to do what is best for him. Obviously if you do not like your children, do not enjoy their talk and company nor answering their questions about the world around them, then you will find it hard work teaching them anything.

The first step of having confidence in one's ability is maybe the hardest, the threshold over which to pass. Almost anyone can teach her child if she believes she can do it, and this confidence in itself helps create the right atmosphere for a child to learn in.

(Throughout all the chapters on education I have made the parent or teacher female and the child male, this being for no other reason than to avoid confusion between he and she, his and her.)

The biggest bonus that parents have to help them in this task is that most children are normally very eager to learn; they want to know how to read or how things work. We all know the multitude of questions that small children ask in their quest for knowledge and understanding of the world about them, the 'how?', 'what for?' and 'why?' Answering such questions can be regarded as one form of teaching, a form that most parents do naturally, although they might not think to call it 'teaching'. Extending this technique to other areas such as reading, writing and mathematics is but a logical step. If parents can feel some of a child's curiosity about the world and have faith in their own abilities, they are a long way on the path to success.

There are many ways that parents can receive help, from books, correspondence courses, educational organisations and schools ashore, all of which make the task easier. In the following chapters some of these sources of help will be discussed, and practical outlines given for parents who want to teach their children on their own.

In the 1960s, there was a movement for deschooling society, which criticised the existing school system and led to the establishment of a number of 'free' or alternative schools. Following on from this some people chose to take their children out of school and teach them at home, various parents fighting long court battles for the right to do so. However, for whatever reasons a child was being taught out of school, and there were many, the interest in home schooling resulted in various books being published and organisations founded, which can also be of interest and help to the sailing parent. One of the leading supporters of home schooling was the late John Holt, teacher and author of many books on educational matters, *How Children Learn* and *How Children Fail* being two of the best known. In his book *Teach Your Own* he suggests that teaching is no mystery, but more a question of commonsense, even though it does involve some real skills, which he outlines more or less as follows:

(1) To help a child learn, one must understand what he already knows and what he does not. This is best accomplished by noting what questions a child asks.
(2) Showing children how to do something is better than telling them how, while letting them do it themselves is even better.
(3) Do not show or tell too much at once, as new ideas are assimilated very slowly and a child has to be sure of a new idea before he can move on to the next.
(4) Give a child as much time as he wants to absorb what he is learning.
(5) Intimidating or frightening children only makes their learning slower and can disrupt it altogether.

Such general principles make sense and the one-to-one ratio that a parent has with her child has many advantages over the situation where a teacher faces a classroom full of pupils. In the first place it is much easier to see quickly that a child does or does not understand a particular point. Then one can either move on straight away to something new instead of doing repetitive examples, or one can take time and deal with any problem the child is having, perhaps preventing its escalation into a greater difficulty. There is a danger in this one-to-one situation of over-teaching, of pushing a child on to more advanced work before he is ready. This is where it is essential to gauge if the child has really understood what he is doing or not, and to let the child set his own pace. Often a child will say whether he wants to go on further or not, so attention should be paid to the child's reaction, although being careful not to let him opt out of work without any good reason.

There are many books on educational theory and it may seem to the layman as though there are just as many theories, so in this chapter I will try to present some of the more important principles involved in education.

The Swiss psychologist Piaget has contributed more than any other person to the modern educational scene. He demonstrated that human development always proceeds in more or less an identical sequence from the simple to the complex. All children broadly follow the same pattern, even if some progress slower and others faster. Part of this development is due to physical change, the gradual maturation of the nervous system as the child grows up. Combined with this maturation are the child's experiences and his interaction with the world around him.

Take a small child playing with differently shaped objects which have to be posted into correctly shaped slots. By the child's own experience of handling the shapes, by trial and error, he learns to identify shapes that are different and how they are different, although he does not know yet the names 'round', 'square' or 'triangular'. The child struggles to adjust his new experiences of these shapes to his previous pattern of thinking, when they were all just pretty coloured objects. This is what Piaget called assimilation and accommodation, which he proposed as the two processes by which a child learns. To illustrate this point we might consider how an adult changes her opinion on some matter. New experiences that she has or things that she reads in the newspaper or events seen on television may build up to the point of assimilation, so that she can only accommodate all these new facts and experiences by altering her opinion on the relevant matter. This is in fact what is happening all the time a child is learning something new.

Every aspect of learning begins with the ordinary concrete experience and only after that is mastered can the child proceed to the corresponding abstraction. For example, only once a child recognises what is round as being a special shape, with a property of roundness all of its own, can he go on to learn that this is described by the word 'round' and eventually develop a permanent notion of roundness.

During this phase of a child's development, the teacher should provide for the child as many real experiences to work from as possible, as regards such concepts as size, colour, weight, and volume.

The mental capacity to deal with these concepts moves in a very definite sequence. If we take the example of size, a child will firstly appreciate this mainly in terms of length and only about a year later also understand it in terms of weight. Much later still comes the ability to comprehend size as an expression of volume or capacity. Particularly in mathematics, textbooks are usually graded very carefully to follow this sequence of children's development, ideas and practice being introduced in the appropriate order.

Children work over their experiences in a kind of digestive process, the understanding coming long before they have the capacity to verbalise or apply it. The child often shows quite clearly by his actions that he understands something, but cannot yet explain it in words. This is clearly seen in language development, a small child understanding much more than he can speak; similarly when we as adults learn another language, we usually understand much more than we can say.

The last stage of intellectual development normally occurs between eleven and fifteen years of age. This is the stage when a child develops the capacity to think and reason beyond his own world and to be able to use symbols and propositions in an abstract way. Only when a child has achieved this level can he comprehend such things as geometrical relationships or understand historical perspectives. This stage brings with it the ability to reason by hypotheses, deductive thinking and a mastery of abstract concepts.

Every child will pass through these definite stages – the brighter ones at an earlier age, others more slowly, while some even as adults will never reach the highest level of abstract reasoning. This development can be accelerated by providing relevant experiences and good teaching.

The concept of 'time' provides a clear example of these stages. At first a child can only relate to the idea of 'before' and 'after' and most parents will have experienced the difficulty of getting a small child to understand that something will happen 'tomorrow'. Then gradually, in the second stage, the child begins to understand the idea of past, present and future. In the third stage a child also comes to understand time in terms such as duration and speed, but only later still when the final stage has been reached is it possible for a child to be taught the subject of history with an understanding of the historical perspective of time. When my son was small he once asked my mother various questions about my father, anxious to find out more about his grandfather. When it was explained that his grandfather had died a long time ago, my son's next question was 'Was he a caveman then?', clearly illustrating his lack of understanding of the perspectives of time.

Teaching has come a long way since the days of memorising and learning everything by rote, when teachers did not care too much if what was taught and learnt was also understood. For a while the pendulum appeared to swing in the other direction, with enthusiastic child-centred educationalists saying that ideas, concepts and intellectual growth would blossom naturally in the minds of curious children if only they were given a suitably rich environment and enough freedom to explore it. The view that concepts will originate spontaneously in the minds of children I believe to be a fallacy, and most teachers now agree that a child's development and learning has to be helped along by teaching. The emphasis in education, however, has shifted into starting from the child's actual experiences, it being the teacher's task to help transform those experiences into understanding by questions, explanations, setting tasks and posing problems, by demonstration and by comment. A teacher, parent or a book is still needed to feed and guide the growth of a child. No amount of theories can change the fact that there are still basic skills to be learnt and knowledge to be acquired, skills and knowledge that will be essential for a useful adult life.

For children, seeing is not only believing; seeing and doing are the kingpins for understanding, a child understanding something much more quickly if he has actually done it or experienced it himself. Children will also learn what interests them for the satisfaction of doing just that and take pride in work well done, the reward being the skill learnt or the work itself. Learning to read is one such skill that most children get great satisfaction out of acquiring for its own sake, for the pleasure of being able to read a book of their own choice right through all by themselves. It is up to the teacher or parent to make the work involved in learning as interesting, challenging and worth doing as she can, neither forcing a child before he is ready nor holding him back from pursuing something that interests him.

True learning that lasts is often that which is self-motivated and self-discovered. When we were sailing in Greece and Turkey, my daughter Doina developed a keen interest in Greek mythology and the tales of the heroes and gods. She read and reread their stories and legends and knew almost every detail of the *Odyssey* by heart. She was seven years old at the time, yet that knowledge remained with her and she was to profit by it years later when coming across classical references in her study of literature at a more advanced level.

Providing children with a stimulating environment is not difficult when cruising, because of the variety of places visited, the closeness to Nature and the experiences that sailing offers. The opportunities for turning these experiences into a voyage of discovery and learning are comparatively easy to find. Education is a continuous process; it does not have to be confined to 'lessons' but can happen at any time or in any place, for knowledge does not fall neatly into separate compartments. When I taught in a London school, it was quite obvious which children had a more stimulating time outside school than others, because quite simply the former had much more to say and write about, more experiences

109

The carvings outside the Tongan Tourist Office are studied by Doina and Ivan as part of their schoolwork.

from which to work. So by providing the stimulation of a new, challenging environment, the sailing parent is already one big step forward.

Parents of older children are often daunted by subjects about which they know little, or subjects such as mathematics which have changed since they themselves were at school. I faced this problem later on in our circumnavigation as my children got older, and I know how difficult it can be. It is not possible to know everything a child wants to know, or to be interested in everything a child is interested in. Nor is it necessarily a help to the child for the parent to try frantically to keep ahead and abreast of all these subjects. In some areas I ended up learning along with the children, but equally I think it is important to be able to admit that one does not know the answer – instead of pretending one does – and then proceed to help the child find out what he wants to know. One of the skills that is an essential part of education is the ability to find the information one needs, knowing how to look up things, use indexes and reference books. This is just as much a part of education – in my opinion maybe more so – as simply giving a child the answer.

The ideas about education that I have written about here are necessarily condensed and also reflect my personal view of some of the principles involved. When I prepared for our voyage, I forced myself to formulate exactly what my own aims were in the education of my children. I knew that I wanted them to be 'educated' in the broadest sense of the word, not just 'schooled'; to be interested in the world we live in, even if they have chosen to be interested in different aspects of it. Also I wanted them to enjoy acquiring knowledge in the way that I had always enjoyed it. My aims were in fact rather lofty and ambitious, and I must confess that on many occasions during those six years of cruising they were lost sight of. Teaching the children was hard work, demanding, occasionally downright boring, and I sometimes took the easiest options in the work I handed out. However, when I look back on that time as a whole, I have no regrets about teaching my children while cruising and am pleased with the results.

As parents we continually take decisions that affect our children's lives and this is particularly apparent when we take them cruising, whether it concerns their physical safety or their education. Children themselves have little choice in the matter and it is difficult for them to realise what is valuable in life, so that the onus of deciding what experiences are valuable and worth pursuing is often on the parent. If the decision is taken to go cruising, it is worth looking at some of the general ideas in education and sorting out one's values and ideas in order to provide some purpose to the venture.

My own stance on education is probably evident in this chapter, but there are many other viewpoints and plenty of stimulating books on this subject which is one that many people feel very strongly about. Of the many parents that I met while cruising who were educating their children, whether using correspondence schools or by themselves, almost all of them took this task very seriously and had given the subject careful thought. Only once or twice did I meet people who failed their children by not making an effort with their education. There may be difficult aspects, hard moments or plain boredom in educating children afloat, but to balance those moments there is certainly a great enjoyment and immense satisfaction to be gained.

Books

Holt, J. (1981) *Teach Your Own*. London: Lighthouse Books.
Kent, G. (1983) *What Should Your Child Know?* London: Harrap.

10
Correspondence Schools and Courses

There are various sources of help available to a parent considering the education of children afloat and a sensible place to seek advice first of all is from the child's present school. The amount of help given will depend on the attitude and interest of individual teachers, but generally teachers and schools are cooperative, suggesting books to use and courses to follow. If one is planning to take a child out of school for a shorter period of time the teacher will often outline what work should be done, maybe even suggesting any special points the child needs to concentrate on. It is wise to continue with the same series of mathematical workbooks or reading scheme that a child is already using, for this will make it easier for him to fit back into his class on his return ashore. Some schools will lend books that the child is currently using, but do make sure that you also lay hands on a teacher's answer book, especially for mathematics, if you want to save yourself some time and effort!

For parents planning a longer cruise there are various correspondence courses and schools that cater for itinerant children or those living in far flung corners of the world. In countries or states where a lot of children live in remote communities and outstations, there are state run correspondence schools, providing a service for these children who do not have access to regular schools. Such correspondence schools are found in several English-speaking countries: Australia, New Zealand, Canada and also in the state of Alaska. These state run schools have an excellent reputation among the yachting families who use them and have the advantage that tuition is usually provided free of charge for citizens or residents of that country. For those people who live in countries or states that do not provide state correspondence schools, there are a number of private correspondence schools available. There is an advantage in taking courses from one's country of origin, because it enables the child to reintegrate more easily into the school system of his own country when necessary.

United States of America

The most well-known of the private correspondence schools worldwide is the Calvert School, which was founded in the last century and has educated tens of thousands of children overseas during the last seventy-five years. As the courses have been designed for children who travel with their parents, or live overseas or in remote places, they can be started at any time of the year and the pupil can work as quickly or as slowly as required. The Calvert courses have been prepared especially for parents with no teaching experience and include a manual which gives precise step by step instructions for the parent as well as other helpful guidance. Approved by the Department of Education of the State of Maryland, the curriculum includes the basic subjects of reading, language skills, composition and mathematics. Other subjects taught are history, geography, history of art and sciences. The school does not offer any foreign languages.

Alongside the actual courses, the Calvert School offers an advisory service for an extra fee, which is strongly recommended by the school. In this service a professional teacher assesses the work that is sent in by the parent, and offers personal guidance, comments and suggestions. If a course is completed satisfactorily by the pupil, this teacher issues a certificate (which is accepted by other schools) that a grade has been successfully completed.

The Calvert School offers courses from first grade through to the eighth grade, and also a kindergarten course for four to five year olds, which has play lessons and emphasises reading and number readiness. The current fees are $200 for the kindergarten, $345 per grade for grades one to four and $370 per grade for grades five to eight. The advisory service varies from $170 to $190 depending on the grade. These fees include the lesson manual, textbooks, workbooks, paper and even supplies such as pencils. Postage by surface mail is included, but if air mail abroad is required an additional $60 to $120 must be paid. As surface mail can easily take up to six weeks to reach a foreign destination, it may be worth paying the extra for air mail or air freight.

Most of the many parents I have talked to using the Calvert School regard it as satisfactory, although Nancy Lewis of *L'Orion* qualified this by saying that, although the courses were good for the earlier grades and basic skills, she felt the higher grades and particularly the sciences needed some supplementing. Most correspondence courses such as those that Calvert offer are flexible, not only as regards the pace of work; they can also be left or picked up again when required, supplemented or only partly used. In Tahiti I met the Samuelsons on *Swan II*, whose daughter Nicky was attending French school ashore in Papeete. Six year old Nicky, already bilingual in French and English, was keeping up with part of the Calvert course she had been studying previously so as to keep her fluency in English while attending French school, illustrating the flexibility with which parents can treat the correspondence courses. It is up to the parent to choose which parts, how much and how fast the course proceeds.

A full list of accredited correspondence schools in the United States can be obtained from the National Home Study Council, 1601 18th Street NW, Washington DC 20009, USA. This council is approved by the US Department of Education as a clearing house for information on home study and as an accrediting agency.

The only accredited school which offers courses from kindergarten right through elementary grades to high school and college education is Home Study International, also approved by the Maryland State Department. Started in 1909, this school is run by the Seventh Day Adventist Church, and although there is an emphasis on Bible studies these are an optional subject.

The elementary programme, from preschool through to grade six, provides all textbooks and materials as well as a parent's guide, which gives instructions and teaching suggestions. At the end of each six week period a test is given in each subject, the tests being returned to the school for grading. Advice is given when needed and a certificate issued on completion of each grade. The courses offered are reading, language, spelling, handwriting, mathematics, social studies, art, music, health, science, physical education and Bible (optional). The total costs of supplies, fees and tuition vary from $299 for the kindergarten to between $515 and $540 per grade for grades one to six if the full course and all textbooks are taken. Shipping or postage costs would have to be added to this.

At junior high school level (grades seven and eight), subjects offered are English, mathematics, social studies, science and health, Bible, and US history. Tuition and supplies are around $150 per subject per grade. At this level there is no parent's guide as the student is expected to be able to use the study guide on his own. This also applies to the high school course (grades nine to twelve), which includes a study guide and all textbooks. Twenty units must be successfully completed to qualify for a high school diploma and these can be selected from a variety of units offered in mathematics, English, business and secretarial, fine arts, health and home economics, history, religion, sciences (biology and chemistry) and languages (French, German and Spanish). The cost is around $200 per unit, for which postage has to be added.

Other accredited correspondence schools which offer the high school diploma only are the American School of Chicago, another long established school used

114

particularly by travelling parents in show business, and the more recently formed Cambridge Academy in North Carolina, the Citizens' High School in Georgia and the International Correspondence School, Newport/Pacific High School in Pennsylvania.

Great Britain

In Great Britain there are neither state nor private correspondence schools for primary or lower secondary aged children, and the nearest equivalent is the Worldwide Education Service (WES) established by the Parents' National Educational Union. This parents' union was founded in 1890 by Charlotte Mason, who believed that parents should play an active role in their children's education – a very advanced view to hold in Victorian England. Charlotte Mason considered that children should be treated as individuals, that education should be an enjoyable process and that parents should also be actively involved in it. For this reason WES tailors its 'Home School' programmes individually for each child, taking into account that child's age and abilities. This is not a correspondence course as such, but more of a guidance service enabling parents to teach their own children. It is designed for parents who have no previous experience of teaching, and has the approval of the British Department of Education and Science.

Each family is allotted a tutor, a qualified teacher, who provides guidance and advice throughout the course. Parents are recommended to visit the organisation in London before they leave and discuss personally with their tutor all their particular educational requirements. The curriculum is designed to enable children to move back easily into the British educational system later on and the textbooks are those in common use in British schools. A French language course is included on cassettes and Latin is also offered as an optional subject. A science kit is available to help overcome the lack of laboratory facilities, but special care has been taken with the science course to include experiments which can be conducted with everyday household items. Music, art and craft are also on the curriculum, as is astronomy. This latter subject only needs a pair of binoculars as equipment, an item that most boats would have. The astronomy cassettes and notes have been written so they can be used to study both the northern and southern hemisphere night skies.

The WES curriculum aims to take advantage of the environment that the child lives in and emphasises the benefits to be gained from studying this. Once a term samples of the child's work are sent to the tutor for assessment and the parent can write for additional help or advice at any time.

Six primary courses are available from five to eleven years and three secondary courses at the senior level from eleven to thirteen plus. There is also a two year nursery course, 'Learning to Learn', which helps develop skills in preparation for primary education. The WES 'Home School' fees vary from £580 per year for age five to £765 per year at the secondary level. The nursery course is £350 for the complete two year course. In addition, approximately £150 a year has to be spent on books and an estimated £120 on postage, which does make WES the most expensive of all the home study schools. As airmail postage is such an expensive item, it is worthwhile collecting as many books as possible before leaving home.

WES does not provide a service beyond the age of fourteen, nor does it prepare children for the General Certificate of Secondary Education (GCSE). However, WES will give advice on suitable courses which do prepare for this examination.

For older children wishing to take public examinations such as GCSE, there are several correspondence schools in Britain, although these are intended primarily for adults. When my daughter was thirteen, I enrolled her in three courses run by the National Extension College in Cambridge. Although designed for adults, Doina had little trouble at that age in following the courses for they were very clearly set out. Similar courses are also run by Wolsey Hall, Oxford, for GCSE, GCE, university degree and certain professional examinations.

The National Extension College courses have their own manuals made up of a series of study units, equivalent to a lecture or class. Each study unit is followed by work to be done by the student. A lot of this work is self-marked, so that a student can tell if he has understood the work correctly. After completing the self-assessment questions, the student's own answers can be compared with the answers and comments written in the manual. This self-assessment is a helpful way of gauging progress without the continual mailing back and forth of material. Every so often in the course there are assignments which have to be returned to be marked by the tutor.

Similarly the Wolsey Hall courses comprise a scheme of study and lesson notes. At the end of each lesson or group of lessons a test is set which is sent to the tutor for assessment. At the end of the subsequent lesson are suggested answers for each preceding test, so the student can monitor his progress. Normally the course notes and suggested answers are sent out at intervals, but it is possible to receive all the material on enrolment if required.

The student on both the National Extension College and Wolsey Hall courses always writes directly to his tutor, who will be a different specialist for each subject studied. This tutor answers any queries and makes comments as well as assessing the student's work.

The wide range of courses offered by these colleges include English language, English literature, French, German, Spanish, Russian, history, geography, sociology, mathematics, biology, physics and chemistry among the many GCSE courses. The advanced ('A') level GCE subjects, which take a student up

116

to the standard required for university entrance, include English literature, French, history, economics, sociology, physics and mathematics. Wolsey Hall has a much wider range at 'A' level and also offers biology, chemistry, German, Italian, Spanish and law.

The courses lead to the GCSE and GCE ('A' level) examinations set by either the University of London or the Associated Examining Board, these two boards being chosen as it is possible to sit their examinations overseas. Both of these boards will give further information about taking examinations abroad on request:

Associated Examining Board, Stag Hill House, Guildford, Surrey GU2 5XJ.
University of London Examination Council, Stewart House, 32 Russell Square, London WC1.

Further information about taking examinations can also be obtained from British Council offices abroad.

The prices of the courses vary, although the majority of National Extension College GCSE courses are around £112 for the complete course and around £112 for 'A' level courses. The Wolsey Hall fees are similar, £105 for GCSE and £110 for 'A' level courses, with mathematical courses being a little more expensive at £120 for GCSE and £140 for 'A' level. These fees do not include the price of essential textbooks which are required for some, but not all, of the courses. Cassettes for the language courses are included. Approximately £20 per course has to be added for postage overseas, but both colleges will continue to tutor free of charge if an examination is failed. Also if within four weeks a student decides a course is too difficult or unsuitable, it may be cancelled and a refund, minus the deposit, is returned to the student.

Australia and New Zealand

Sailing parents from Australia and New Zealand are among the luckiest worldwide, being able to take advantage of state run correspondence schools, where tuition is provided free of charge to residents. In Australia the Department of Education of every state, with the exception of the small area covered by the Capital Territory, runs a correspondence school. For over fifty years these schools have catered mainly for children in remote farms and cattle stations, aiming to give the same standard of education as that received by children in state schools. The courses offered range from preschool through primary to the secondary level up to the Higher School Certificate.

The primary and secondary correspondence schools run by the State of Queensland have successfully tutored many sailing children over the years and

117

Ben Lucas (9) has never been to school ashore. For five years he has been taught by the Queensland correspondence school, while accompanying his parents on a world voyage on *Tientos*.

have been particularly recommended to me by Australians using them. At the primary level the work is done in exercise books or workbooks provided by the school and instruction papers are included in the package. These exercises have to be returned to the school for marking, there being thirty-six weekly papers in the first three years and eighteen fortnightly papers in the second three. However, there is no set period of time to complete the work and the child can proceed at his own pace, although children are expected to put in about four to five hours a day, five days a week.

The secondary school offers a wide range of subjects including several foreign languages, sciences, typewriting, shorthand and accounting as well as mathematics, English, history and geography. Again there are no fees for tuition or lesson materials, although some textbooks and stationery will have to be bought. Postage has to be paid when material is sent overseas, although not within Australia. The school makes extensive use of cassettes, not only in languages but also in other subjects. A descant recorder is required for the music course, and also access to a piano or other keyboard instrument, which might be a little difficult when cruising, although a small portable electronic keyboard could provide the solution. Kits are available for the science courses, but cannot be sent overseas, so these would have to be picked up before leaving Australia.

The Australian family, the van Zelderens, have used the Queensland correspondence schools for eight years while sailing on their 41 foot ketch *White Pointer*. With one circumnavigation and over 90,000 sea miles behind them, fourteen year old Edith and sixteen year old Ronald van Zelderen have completed almost their entire education afloat, being six and eight years old when they started cruising. When I met them in Raiatea in the Society Islands, Ronald was preparing for his School Certificate examinations, which he was hoping to take at an Australian consulate or embassy. He was studying a wide range of subjects, including French and several scientific subjects. The children's mother, Maria van Zelderen, was very satisfied with the correspondence school, but pointed out that it was essential never to let the work fall behind. The system itself was very good, Maria told me, but everything depended on the student and the amount of effort he or she put into the courses. The van Zelderen children studied for about five to six hours a day in port, but rather less at sea, depending very much on the weather. To stop them distracting one another, Maria made sure that they did their schoolwork in separate cabins.

The correspondence school run by New Zealand's Department of Education has a similar history to the Australian schools in providing an excellent education for isolated or travelling children over the last sixty years. Approval for enrolment has to be received from the Department of Education, but is normally given to New Zealand citizens or residents who intend their children to continue in the New Zealand system of education. There are no fees although postage overseas has to be paid. Some equipment for science subjects and library books are not sent overseas.

A full range of courses is offered up to University Entrance, although due to demand at home the preschool programme for under fives is not available overseas. The courses are flexible and many combinations are possible, especially at the secondary level. The school aims at providing friendly tuition and maintains a one-to-one relationship between the child and his teacher by an exchange of letters and tapes.

In the primary section the work is divided into sets of lessons, each set comprising approximately two weeks' work. A booklet is provided for parents, which gives guidance on the supervision of lessons and how extra help can be given to the child. The number of hours expected to be worked varies from fifteen hours per week for the five year olds up to twenty-six hours per week for the older pupils. In the secondary section pupils can choose from a wide range of subjects within the fields of English, mathematics, art, commerce, languages, home economics, music, sciences, social sciences, technicraft, clothing and textiles, leading to the School Certificate examination in form five. Similar choices in forms six and seven lead to the Sixth Form Certificate, Higher School Certificate and University Entrance if required. Arrangements to sit these external examinations have to be made well in advance because it entails finding both a suitable location such as an embassy or school and a suitable person to supervise the examination.

Canada

Education in Canada is the responsibility of the government of each province and details of correspondence courses can be obtained from the Department of Education in the province where one resides. The British Columbia Correspondence School is used by many sailing families. To enrol in the school, proof is needed of residence in British Columbia and it is essential to have a permanent address in the province to which school material will be sent. It is the responsibility of the parents to arrange for the forwarding of this material. Registration fees vary from Can. $18 for the kindergarten to Can. $29.50 for grades one to seven and Can. $23.50 for each of the secondary school courses. In addition some textbooks have to be purchased and postage paid. Tapes are supplied for the language and shorthand courses, as is some laboratory equipment for certain science courses.

The kindergarten course includes a week-to-week teaching guide with ideas for activities to help the child's development. The courses for grades one to seven incorporate mathematics, language arts, social studies, general science and art. There are no choices and the courses are based on the course of study in general use in British Columbian schools. A timetable is supplied which the child is expected to adhere to.

For grades eight to twelve there is an increasing number of choices as the student progresses, although some courses under the headings of English, mathematics, social studies and science remain compulsory. Apart from these subjects at grades eleven and twelve level there is a choice from among forty different subjects of which nine courses must be chosen. A Senior Secondary School certificate is awarded when graduation requirements have been fulfilled and the requisite number of courses completed satisfactorily.

General points

All the correspondence schools are very helpful and aware of the special needs and problems of their pupils. Much of the choice of course will depend on one's nationality, for clearly it is an advantage to take a course from one's own country. Some parents may want to do so just for that reason – that their children may keep in touch with their own roots and history, while travelling to places of other traditions and cultures. The basic skills of language and mathematics, however, are treated similarly by all the schools, so there is no reason why another country's school cannot be used if the courses are more easily obtained or regarded as more suitable or more reasonably priced. In fact WES have tutored American children, and plenty of other nationalities have used the Calvert School. Not only the suitability of a course but also the expenses have to be considered, and one of the highest expenses is that of postage. For that reason alone it might be worth picking up an entire year's course when one is in a particular country.

A reliable mailing address is essential, for the problem of receiving mail when one is continually on the move is one of the drawbacks of the correspondence courses. There is nothing more infuriating than having to delay a departure and wait in some foreign port for the mail to arrive, as I have watched other parents do. An alternative is to take delivery of complete courses before leaving home. Mailing addresses worldwide vary in their reliability and large packets of books or cassettes are much more likely to disappear en route than ordinary letters. General Delivery (poste restante) is used by most yachts, and this is an excellent service in many countries though extremely poor in others, notably Bali, Central America and the French territories such as Tahiti and Martinique, where mail is returned after fourteen days if not claimed. Yacht Clubs, Harbour Masters and American Express offices are other alternatives to be used in places where the post office is unreliable. The Seven Seas Cruising Association, PO Box 1598, Fort Lauderdale, Florida 33302, USA, has a list of contact addresses around the world for the use of both full and associate members of the Association. Similar services are now offered by other offshore cruising clubs such as The Ocean Cruising Club of Great Britain or the Trans-Ocean Club of Germany. The best address to use for a particular place can often be found out in advance by the cruising grapevine or via amateur radio networks.

Another difficulty associated with mailing is that children do not relate easily

Colette Boete helps her grandchildren Gaelle (9) and Loic (6) with their lessons from the French state correspondence school.

121

to work they have done some time previously when it is returned with corrections or comments after several weeks or sometimes even months. This applies especially to the younger children, but even older ones may have some difficulty remembering all the details of work done long ago.

As the correspondence courses are designed for children living on land, some parents have complained that many of the suggestions and topics are difficult to follow, whether it is studying the earthworm, making a traffic survey or getting access to a piano. With a little ingenuity such items can be adapted or changed, but this is one of the reasons why some parents teach their children on their own without the aid of one of the correspondence schools.

Among the families I have met while cruising or interviewed for surveys, approximately half of the children of school age were being educated using one or other of the correspondence courses, usually but not always from their country of origin. The other fifty per cent were being taught by their parents without using a correspondence course, although often with books sent from their home country.

Useful addresses

United States of America

American School, 875 East 58th Street, Chicago, Illinois 60611.

Calvert School, 105 Tuscany Road, Baltimore, Maryland 21210.

Cambridge Academy, Petti Building, Suite B, PO Box 1289, Banner Elk, North Carolina 28604.

Citizens' High School, 5582 Peachtree Road, Suite 107, Atlanta, Georgia 30341.

Home Study International, 6940 Carroll Avenue, Takoma Park, Maryland 20912.

ICS-Newport/Pacific High School, Scranton, Pennsylvania 18515.

Great Britain

National Extension College, 18 Brooklands Avenue, Cambridge CB2 1BR.

Wolsey Hall, 99 Banbury Road, Oxford, OX2 6PR.

Worldwide Education Service, Strode House, 44-50 Osnaburgh Street, London, NW1 3NN.

Australia

Correspondence School, 405 Montague Road, West End, Queensland 4101.

Distance Education Centre, Parliament Place, West Perth, Western Australia 6005.

Correspondence School, GPO Box 7098, Sydney, New South Wales, 2001.

New Zealand

Correspondence School, 11 Portland Crescent, Thorndon, Private Bag, Wellington.

Canada

Ministry of Education, Correspondence Education Branch, 617 Government Street, Victoria, British Columbia, V8V 4W6.

Ministry of Education, Communication Services Branch, Mowat Block, Queen's Park, Toronto, Ontario, M7A 1L2.

11
Schools Ashore

Nearly all sailing parents send their children to schools ashore when a stay in port is long enough to justify it. This may be the ideal solution for parents who are having any problems teaching their children, especially in the early stages. A longer stay in one place can even be planned into a cruise to allow a child to spend some time in school. Although providing a welcome rest from the daily chore of teaching or supervising correspondence course work, the main reason why parents choose to send their children to school ashore is the chance it gives them to mix and make contact with other children of their own age.

In spite of the increase in families cruising, the relative scarcity of other children is one of the drawbacks to lengthy voyages. So it is not surprising that when families with similar aged children meet up, they often cruise in company for a while. As a result of their peripatetic life, sailing children are usually outgoing and make friends at lightning speed, aware that time is short and that they will soon be on the move again. This applies particularly to making friends with children on other cruising boats, for all these children live in the same world, have had similar experiences and express similar needs. There is an unspoken bond which draws them together. On the other hand some sailing children find that they make friends with children who live ashore rather more slowly, especially the older children who may have become more self-conscious and inhibited. Many of these older children do not easily reintegrate into school life ashore, finding themselves different to other children, as a result of living in a more adult environment. Also sailing children are often used to a lot more autonomy and freedom than their counterparts in schools ashore and can find these schools difficult to fit in to, especially those with a more authoritarian atmosphere. Younger children lack some of these problems and usually take to school ashore as an interesting adventure like the rest of their lives.

Among the parents subscribing to correspondence courses, a minority do not send their children to school ashore at all, saying that they do not want to interrupt the course unnecessarily. If the child is preparing for examinations at a more senior level, this obviously makes sense. One American couple I met, who were cruising in the Pacific, only sent their child ashore in English speaking countries and kept on with the correspondence course in other places. However, many parents profit by the opportunity that a longer stay in a foreign country offers as a chance for their children to learn an additional language. It is remarkable how many of the children on long distance cruising boats speak more than one language, often quite fluently and at a younger age than when normally taught in school. This occasionally results in some unusual accents, my own children for a while speaking French with a definite Polynesian lilt, while the French children Sidonie and Fabien of *Calao* spoke English with a strong Australian accent and matching colloquial vocabulary. Together the four children conversed in the most atrocious mixture of both languages quite happily.

French teenager Corinne Martin of *El Djezair* had spent five years cruising and thought that the chance this had given her to learn English and Spanish was one of the benefits of the sailing life. She enjoyed learning languages and had made an effort to do this in all the different countries where her family had cruised. Six year old Nicky Samuelson of *Swan II*, whose mother is French and father English, was already bilingual in these languages and had also learned some Spanish while cruising in Mexico and Central America. In Tahiti, Nicky was attending a French school ashore, but also still doing half of her Calvert School course to keep her English language skills up to scratch. A correspondence course should be flexible enough to allow this, although a few schools do require the work to be mailed in at regular intervals within the school year.

Also in Tahiti, where many long distance cruising yachts make a stop of several months, another couple took their young two year old son regularly to the day care facility for preschool children, making an effort so that he met and played with children of his own age. This is especially important for only children, who stand in danger of becoming isolated and lonely on board a boat, confident in their dealings with adults but lacking social skills in mixing with their own age group.

In my experience schools ashore are very welcoming to travelling children and I have not heard of any cases where children were not accepted into a local school temporarily. All the schools I have approached have been extremely accommodating and made every effort to see that my children fitted in. Doina and Ivan spent two terms in school in New Zealand during the summer we passed there

On remote Pitcairn Island, the small school welcomes Doina and Ivan, increasing its roll from eight to ten.

avoiding the hurricane season in the South Pacific. This was a very valuable experience for it was long enough for them to get some real worth out of the experience and also gave me a yardstick against which to measure the results of my teaching. Earlier they had spent a month in French school in the Gambier Islands, which had worked wonders for their French. They had been a little diffident about enrolling in this school, but as French was not the mother tongue of the Polynesian children of the island either, they soon realised that they were at no disadvantage. Schools teaching in English, however, are to be found throughout the world and it is the language of education in many countries in the Caribbean and Pacific.

My children have spent as little as a few days at schools on Aitutaki in the Cook Islands, Dregerhaven in Papua New Guinea, and even one day on Pitcairn Island. In these small remote communities, the local teachers were as pleased to accept the children into their classes as I was to send them, regarding Doina and Ivan as a stimulating presence for their own children, who had seen little of the outside world. In all of these places it invariably meant that Doina and Ivan arrived home from their first day at school with several new friends in tow who wanted to come and inspect our boat.

While the island children were interested in our boat and the life we led, in return my children enjoyed visiting their homes ashore and partaking of their

126

On Nukulaelae in Tuvalu, Doina is taught how to weave a crown of frangipani flowers.

way of life, learning how to grate coconut and make cream, plait frangipani flowers into garlands or sail an outrigger canoe. In Malaysia, virtually adopted by the family of the caretaker of the Perak Yacht Club, they became adept at eating with chopsticks and playing Chinese card games. Above all, everywhere we sailed they learnt that children are similar the whole world over, enjoy the same jokes, and play almost identical games, regardless of what language they speak or the colour of their skin.

Later on in our voyage as Doina became a teenager, she did ask us not to send her to schools ashore, preferring to carry on with school on board. This was partly because she found parting from her new friends to be increasingly painful. 'As soon as I settle in and make good friends, I have to say goodbye,' she complained. 'I prefer not to do it, then I won't be disappointed when we sail on.'

The need for friends of the same age is particularly acute among teenagers, who can find spending virtually 24 hours a day in the company of their parents and other adults very frustrating. Also their education at this age does become very demanding and complicated if one tries to offer the same wide range of subjects as schools ashore. Many families resolve this, as we did, by planning to end their cruise when their children reach the senior or secondary level, so they can complete their education ashore. Other parents try to resolve the problem by dispatching their teenage children home to attend school, often sending them to stay with grandparents, while the parents continue cruising. This has varying results, the separation of children and parents after a close family life together not always being successful.

One New Zealand couple I met while they were sailing in European waters had increasing difficulty in getting their teenage son to apply himself to his schoolwork, so that eventually they sent him home ahead of themselves to attend school. When I met them several years later in New Zealand, they were very disappointed because he had never managed to catch up with his age group and had left school discontented, with a feeling of inferiority. Lis and Yves Boucher of *Farewel* encountered similar problems. For the first part of their world voyage they had educated their two teenage children using the French state correspondence school. Not satisfied with the results, they then decided to send their children back to boarding schools in France to study for their final examinations. The Bouchers planned their cruising carefully so that they were in convenient places for the children to fly out and join them during school vacations. This arrangement worked for a while, but was less than ideal, Lis particularly not enjoying the cruising life without her children. In the end the Bouchers sold *Farewel* in Singapore and returned to shore life.

Many of the decisions regarding older children must take into account what the children themselves want to do with their lives. If a child has a particular job or career in mind, it might be necessary for examinations to be taken, so that he can enter the appropriate training course or higher education, and this should be borne in mind. Some parents slow their cruising down in order to spend several months at a time in port so that their children can go to school, but this has its problems if the school system is different to that of their country of origin or previous schools attended. Children of this older age group often have their own definite opinions on the subject of schools ashore or afloat, and if they decide to remain afloat and stay with correspondence courses, they should be prepared for the self-discipline that will be required for work at this senior level.

The problems concerned with the education of older children are often deciding factors in ending a cruise and moving back ashore, parents not wanting to deny their children the chance of deciding their own future, keeping their options open and not closing the door on possibilities. This was the prime reason why we interrupted our cruising life and moved ashore after six years of sailing the oceans of the world.

On our return to shore life, it was the social reintegration into school that my children found the most difficult, rather than the academic side. Similar difficulties were experienced by almost all of my cruising friends who took a similar course. Cruising children are usually obviously different to the rest of their classmates – for instance, not knowing anything about television programmes or pop stars. Ivan was looked at most strangely when, after being asked which football team he supported, it became apparent that he did not·

know the name of a single team. In the beginning both my children even tried to conceal the fact that they had sailed around the world, in an attempt to be like everyone else and belong to the group. Gradually with time this problem resolved itself; they made friends and settled in, learning all the necessary cultural requirements of football teams, pop stars and television programmes.

Neither Doina nor Ivan had any problems with the schoolwork, being if anything ahead not behind their age group when they returned to school in England. The six years spent sailing, being educated afloat either by myself, in schools in various parts of the world, or with correspondence courses, had only had a positive effect on their education. The families that I have kept in touch with around the world all report a similar initial difficulty with social reintegration, but few problems with the actual work. It seems that sailing children take school and work more seriously when they have been outside the system for a while.

While sailing, the twin problems of education and the lack of contact with other children have to be resolved, and the two problems often go hand in hand. Schools ashore serve their purpose in this respect, especially for the younger child, for they give a change of teacher and viewpoint, offer contact with other children, and the stimulation of different subjects and even different languages. For the older teenage child, the advantages of the social contact have to be weighed against the educational interruption. As in many other aspects of cruising, the best solution will depend on the individual child and the long term plans of the family.

12
Teaching a Child Oneself

A considerable number of cruising parents, myself included, decide to educate their children themselves and not follow a set correspondence course. There are many individual reasons for this choice, a major one being that the child's work can be marked, commented on and corrected on the spot, which is bound to be more productive than waiting for mail to be returned. This is especially valid for younger children. For those on a limited budget, the cost of correspondence courses for a couple of children of different ages, plus the cost of postage, can also be another major factor in the decision. A further point in favour of a personal education is that it can be tailored to take full advantage of the rich, stimulating environment that cruising offers. I believe that at its best this can give a greater breadth of education than is found in the average school. Apart from this breadth, if the child's interest is aroused by his immediate experiences, by what he has seen and done, it is much more likely that this learning will also be retained for a longer time. This applies particularly to older children, who can benefit fully from all that a voyage offers.

However, if parents find this task is too difficult and they are not happy teaching their children themselves, there are always the other two alternatives – to stop for longer periods of time in ports where the child can attend a school ashore or to subscribe to a correspondence course. This might be particularly relevant for the first year so that a child understands what school is all about and makes a start on reading, writing and mathematics. The parent might feel more able to take over once the child has mastered the basic skills.

Organisation and routine

Although rewarding in the long run, the daily task of educating one's child is a demanding one. The first step in easing this task is one of organisation. Whether a correspondence course or a more individual education is followed, some of the difficulties are the same, mainly to do with discipline and routine. A regular timetable is essential as a check that an equal emphasis is given to all the major subjects and that no subject is neglected or given too much attention. As well as being one way of combating the many distractions that occur while cruising, children may also feel more secure when working within a regular framework. And last but not least it removes part of that otherwise recurring question, 'What shall we do today?'

The first decision is how much time to spend on school. With the one-to-one relationship of teacher and pupil and the amount of 'education' that will be going on outside of the floating classroom, not nearly so much time need be spent on schoolwork as in school ashore. In the large classes of most schools, so much time is wasted in other matters that the amount of actual learning time per day is very small. If a child has not understood something, he might have to wait to catch the teacher's attention, or alternatively, if he works quickly, he might have to sit doing nothing, waiting for others to finish. The age of the child will also be a deciding factor in the amount of time spent, as younger children have a shorter concentration span. Up to the age of seven, I think that little more than one hour per day is necessary, maybe in shorter half-hour periods. Over that age, two hours is probably sufficient until the secondary level is reached (around eleven or twelve), when this could be increased to three hours. Apart from older children studying for examinations, there is no reason why school should take longer than three hours a day, unless of course a child is following up something out of his own interest, when he should never be discouraged. This may well happen when the subject matter is more exciting, relevant and chosen by the child himself. Some activities, which are included in a school programme ashore, whether reading a particular book, art and craft work, or exercising a foreign language, will often take place outside of the school timetable and not be labelled or regarded as 'schoolwork'.

A short break of a quarter of an hour or so should be taken between each hour's work, or the work can be split into morning and afternoon. Personally I am in favour of getting all schoolwork done in the morning so as to leave the afternoon free. For similar reasons it is a good idea to have no school on Saturday and Sunday, making a break between each week. One of the big advantages of home school is undoubtedly its flexibility and in the free life that sailing offers, it would be foolish to be a complete slave to a timetable or routine. If something exciting happens or the weather is really rotten, the timetable should be thrown overboard, at least until the interesting event, storm or whatever the distraction

131

was, has passed over. There is no reason why Monday's timetable cannot be rerun on Saturday.

My children sometimes chose to work through Saturdays and Sundays while we were on a long passage, and then have a holiday from school when we reached port. Many parents alter their routine at sea, depending both on the weather and whether their children suffer from seasickness or not. Many cruising children do work harder when at sea, partly as one way of keeping boredom at bay. On the other hand, some children do virtually no work at all while on passage, but work harder in port. Each family has to decide what routine is best for them.

The timetable

The composition of the timetable should give precedence to the basic skills of mathematics and of language (reading and writing). For a young child, the daily timetable would consist typically of a reading lesson, arithmetic or number work, drawing and writing. This is all that needs to be done as actual schoolwork, for much of a child's education at a younger age occurs through his experiences outside the classroom and the questions he asks about the world around him. For example, walking along a beach, picking up shells and studying them, and later looking in a book to find out their names, is as much education as anything learnt sitting down at a table. Much of a child's creative work at a younger age will consist of drawing and writing about what he has seen or done.

With older children, the timetable should similarly never neglect the basic skills, mathematics and language skills being the most important. The other subjects can vary and it is a good idea to change them periodically, dropping one subject for a month or two and including another. Our own timetable varied quite a lot depending on where we were, especially as regards subjects like history or geography. Scientific subjects should also be included in the curriculum from the wide range of topics that science encompasses, from nature study to human biology, simple chemistry and physics. Astronomy and navigation are two subjects that could be included, which have a particular relevance to the cruising life, as would marine biology. Artistic expression, whether in art or craft work or music, can have a place on the curriculum, although these subjects can equally well be pursued outside of school hours, as long as they are not neglected. I always kept one period of time free on the last day of the week's timetable, either to follow up a subject I felt needed extra work or, if this was not necessary, for the children to choose something that they enjoyed studying.

Once a timetable has been created, it is important to try to stick to it. Discipline is quite difficult to maintain on a boat, where distractions are forever cropping up, visitors arrive or an enticing beach is just a short swim away. It is essential to be firm – to tell visitors that school is in progress, or to try to remove

Examples of timetables

7 to 10 year old child

1st hour	Mathematics	English (creative writing)	Mathematics	Science or nature study	Mathematics
2nd hour	Handwriting practice English (vocabulary, spelling)	Mathematics	Environmental or social studies (history, geography)	English (reading, comprehension)	Free choice

12 to 14 year old child

1st hour	Mathematics	English (creative writing)	Science	Mathematics	French or other language
2nd hour	English (reading, comprehension book reviews)	Mathematics	English (continue writing or word study vocabulary, grammar)	Science	Mathematics
3rd hour	French or other language	Environmental or social studies (history, geography)	Environmental or social studies (history, geography)	English (literature)	Free choice

some of the distractions by keeping the children away from vantage points. For this reason I rarely let my children study on deck, but always ran school below, where they could not so easily watch the activity going on in a particular port or anchorage. Firmly refusing to let the children play until after school is finished is easier to accomplish when any other children on nearby boats are also doing schoolwork at the same time. A little parental cooperation among boats in such a case is worthwhile for all concerned, for there is nothing that destroys concentration quicker than a gang of children playing in the near vicinity.

It is not easy playing the role of teacher in addition to that of parent, especially as regards discipline over schoolwork. Children do not regard mother or father with the same attitude as they do a teacher in school, the relationship lacking a certain seriousness and respect because it is by its nature already much more intimate. This cannot be resolved completely, but can be helped by parents trying to make a difference between the time when they are being teachers and when they are being parents.

A step towards achieving this separation is by creating a definite classroom atmosphere. Work should be done in the same place at the same time every day. If possible, the child's own cabin or a corner of the main cabin should be designated as the school area. A table is obviously needed for writing on and a separate locker can be reserved for school books and other items. Near this school area some portion of a bulkhead might be kept for displaying some of the child's work, such as a drawing, piece of writing or poem. Displaying work gives a child pride in that work as work well done, which is a reward in itself.

If there is more than one child, the question of them distracting each other must be considered and it may be necessary to separate them into different study areas. Sometimes, however, it is useful to be able to teach them together to save one's own time, even if they are of different ages, unless those ages are very far apart. For example, if writing is on the timetable, one might plan a particular topic such as poems about animals. Some poems could be read aloud, both children discussing them and saying what they liked or disliked about the poems, talking about the descriptive words used by the poets, and so on. Then each child could attempt his own animal poem at his own level. The essential thing is not to compare directly what they have written but to discuss each child's efforts separately. With two children on board, distractions can be reduced and the teacher's life made easier if the timetable is planned so that the children are doing similar subjects at the same time. Some thought may have to be given to setting one child work he can get on with alone while attention is paid to the other one and vice versa.

There is no reason why both parents should not be involved in the teaching process, especially if their talents lie in different directions. One parent might supervise the language and writing skills while the other, with more mathematical capabilities, might deal with mathematics and sciences. If one parent has musical talents or linguistic abilities, obviously he or she could teach just those particular subjects, even if not involved with the rest of schoolwork.

It is not easy to teach a foreign language if one does not speak it oneself, but fortunately there are cassettes, which can help foster correct pronunciation. Many cruising children learn other languages simply by meeting and playing with children of other nationalities or by attending schools ashore. For younger children it is best to keep any language work on an oral level, with maybe some simple writing, leaving the study of grammar or syntax until they are older. This way they learn to speak the language the natural way that we all learn our own native tongues.

Occasionally it is possible to enlist the skills of other people in the cruising fraternity. Cruising in company with the French Bouteleux family of *Calao*, we sometimes swapped our two elder children, who were more advanced in their

134

language studies. I would make conversation in English with Sidonie and listen to her read, while my friend Muriel did the same thing for my daughter Doina in French. Similarly Doina took her writing and poetry one afternoon to show to Bill Stocks of *Kleena Kleene II*, when we were anchored close together in Papua New Guinea. An experienced teacher with a Master's degree in English, Bill was able to give Doina valuable advice on her work that she still remembers today. Wintering in Cyprus, Sandra Crowhurst of *Twin Melody* wrote to tell me how lucky she was with her neighbours in the marina, 'a French couple of proxy-grandparents who give the children French lessons three times a week'. The cruising fraternity encompasses people of many different professions and talents and, with the camaraderie of the sea, they will often be only too happy to be consulted and to give advice if asked.

Teaching a child to play a musical instrument is very difficult if one is unable to play oneself, as I know only too well. But if a child shows a desire to learn, a recorder is a small instrument ideal for a beginner, robust and easy to find space for on a boat, and for which there are simple self-tuition books. If a parent does play an instrument of any kind and has it on board, passing on this ability to his or her child should present few problems. Listening to music figures prominently among the pastimes of cruising families, particularly on passage, so that even if not making music, a child can easily be given plenty of opportunity to listen to and appreciate music of different kinds.

Neither music nor art and craft would I place as allotted hours on the school timetable, for these subjects can easily be catered for in the children's leisure time. Paint, especially powder paint mixed with water, can be very messy to deal with on a boat. It is probably better to encourage the child to use coloured pencils, crayons or felt tipped pens for colouring, although block water colours could be used under supervision. Wax crayons can also get rather sticky in hot climates, although they are good for rubbings. Other suggestions for artistic expression suitable for the confines of a boat are modelling with plasticine or modelling clay, or making collages with cut-out magazine pictures, Christmas cards, pieces of fabric, silver foil, seeds, leaves – anything in fact that can be glued on paper or, better still, on card. Papercraft, using coloured paper which can be cut or folded to make silhouettes or friezes, is another idea. Models can be made out of cardboard boxes, plastic containers and other junk, wide sticky paper tape being excellent for this. Woodwork, kite making, or jewellery making from small shells, are other suggestions in the craft field. It is wise to keep a close eye on any use of glue, paint or crayons, maybe confining it to one area, workbench or table covered with something to protect it.

Keeping records

It is not only the children that need the organised routine of a timetable and planned work, but also the parents, especially as school afloat is by its nature so flexible. For this reason some form of keeping records of what one has done is vital, not only to gauge the actual work completed and the child's progress, but because it may be necessary at a later date to produce some evidence of a child's work to a school or educational authority when one returns ashore.

Jeff Macdonald with his parents Liz and Bruce on *Horizon*. During their circumnavigation Jeff's education was devised and carried out entirely by Liz.

These records can be quite simple – a calendar with the number of working days ticked off. Results of work completed and marks in any tests can be recorded along with comments on the child's work or progress, even remarks about his attitude or interest in the work he is doing. These brief notes not only help to assess progress, but enable one to check that no important topic has been neglected or forgotten. The records will also help indicate when it is time to move on to something new.

Recording notes on the curriculum also ensures that in subjects like mathematics the logical sequence of steps is followed. In many areas certain skills or facts have to be learnt and mastered before one can move on to the next step. These basic forms of understanding do not just come along on their own; rather, education is a long-term process of building block upon block towards an objective, in which the organisation of the curriculum and timetable are some of the tools used.

In the chapters that follow on teaching reading, writing and mathematics, the emphasis is on the earlier years and younger children. This is mainly because I have found that parents of younger children are more likely to attempt to educate their children themselves than the parents of older children, when the subject matter and syllabus become more complicated. Nearly all the parents of teenagers that I have met cruising have used correspondence courses, schools ashore or have called a temporary halt to their cruising. Some relevant points, however, have been included for older children as well, especially where this can help a parent supervising or assessing progress on a correspondence course or providing additional tutoring. The general suggestions will, I hope, be applicable to all subjects and all ages, for these concern attitudes of mind and ways of approaching education, whichever path one follows.

Support groups

Several organisations have been formed by parents who have taken their children out of the school system or by educators such as John Holt who believed strongly in home schooling. Although these organisations are mostly concerned with land based families, they can provide support, ideas and encouragement for sailing families as well.

Education Otherwise of Great Britain, publishes a bimonthly newsletter and various other small booklets, such as a guide to home-based education or suggestions for learning at home for the under-twelves. Advice on specific matters and exchange of information is available to members, as is an information resource centre, which issues a guide to books and other suitable educational materials.

The American Growing without Schooling, started by John Holt, also publishes bimonthly newsletters for home schoolers. Both of these newsletters contain, among other items, practical suggestions, ideas and tips that other parents have found successful; reviews of books, courses, reading schemes, etc. and useful addresses for other source material. Back issues of the newsletters are available from both organisations. Many of the publications and newsletters are also on sale to non-members.

In conclusion, some form of timetable and daily routine is necessary in order to keep a balance between subjects and prevent the long-term aims being lost sight of. Some child-centred educationalists have gone too far in the other direction, recommending that no set curriculum or timetable is necessary. In my opinion it takes a very exceptional teacher to work in this kind of free state and the majority of us cruising parents have few pretensions to being so exceptional, so we need a guiding framework to work within as much as our children do. When talking to other parents educating their children afloat, whether by themselves or by correspondence courses, keeping to a daily routine and a definite timetable was pointed out by nearly all of them as an absolute necessity. However, the discipline involved in keeping to this routine was considered by all parents to be one of the most difficult and trying aspects of education afloat. That does not mean that if a child is enthusiastically engrossed in a piece of work, such as writing a story, one should stop him just because the hour is up. One of the joys of teaching afloat is that the bells which ring on board have nothing to do with school.

Useful addresses

Education Otherwise, 25 Common Lane, Hemingford Abotts, Cambridgeshire PE18 9AN, England.

Growing without Schooling, Holt Associates, 729 Boylston Street, Boston, Massachusetts, 02116, USA.

13
Learning to Read

Without doubt the ability to read easily and fluently is the lynchpin of education, for not only does reading unlock the doors to knowledge, but it is also a source of great pleasure in itself. The ability to read well is essential for progress in all other subjects, from mathematics to history, so acquiring this skill must take priority in the early years. When cruising with young children, at some point it is vital that parents encourage and help their children to learn to read or prepare them for it. If the child has already started reading when the cruise begins, the growth of his skills in reading must not be neglected either, for there is still a lot to be improved upon once the basic technique has been mastered.

Because of the essential nature of reading and the pleasure it can bring, it is very important not to destroy this pleasure by pushing too hard and too early. Failure in the early stages can have disastrous consequences and inhibit the child's further progress. In the one-to-one relationship there is always a danger of overteaching by a parent anxious for the child to succeed, and this must be borne in mind. On the other hand children who are taught with a low pupil-teacher ratio have been found to read on average earlier than those in large classes. All children are different, in their rate of physical maturation, their intellectual capacity and their span of concentration and interest, so it is wise to let them set the pace. A child will soon say if he wants to learn more or not and will develop his own rate of working. It is quite normal for some children to be late starters, particularly active boisterous boys who have little time for sitting still and concentrating. Until a child is about seven years old there is no need for anxiety if he cannot read, and indeed in some countries school only begins at this age.

Most children, however, will want to learn long before this and many are successful fluent readers before seven. The teaching of reading is probably one of the subjects most researched and written about and there are shelves of books on this subject as well as almost as many methods and techniques. In spite of this, no one method has been proven to be the only, correct or perfect way and different methods work well with different teachers and different children. In fact most normal children will learn to read no matter what method is used and even in spite of a poor teacher. This should encourage the parent daunted by this seemingly difficult task, even though a few children do experience real difficulties which will be discussed later. Many of the problems that occur in schools do not apply to the floating classroom. In school, a teacher has to cope with so many children at different stages and of varying abilities, that often a child fails or falters only because his individual differences are not catered for. Therefore the sailing parent will start with a big advantage in that she can follow the progress of her own child at a natural pace, dealing with any difficulties as soon as they arise. Learning to read should be as natural as learning to walk and to talk. A parent teaches her child to talk by talking and listening; in a similar way, reading is taught by reading and listening.

Ready for reading

The first requirement is that a child is ready to begin. A lot has been written about 'reading readiness', but there is no one magic moment to be caught for each child; it is just a matter of commonsense. Obviously for a child to read with meaning there has to be a certain maturity of the nervous system. The child should have a reasonable vocabulary and developed language, for a beginner cannot be expected to read words he does not know. Secondly, he should have normal eyesight and hearing, so that he can discriminate between visual and auditory symbols. He should also possess a certain coordination between eye and brain, so that these function together. To illustrate this, a child looking at a picture should be able to point out and name objects and colours and say what is happening in the picture. In matching games such as dominoes, he should be able to match the like patterns successfully. The child should be able to differentiate between different shapes, letters and words and pick out the same shape from a group of similar shapes such as in those examples given below. A child unable to do this will not be able to differentiate words well enough to read them.

△	○	△	▢	◇	▽
ჼ	8	W	Ɛ	≥	3
d	p	b	g	a	d
dog	god	big	dog	pod	bog

In the auditory field the child should be able to repeat letter sounds and words, distinguish between different sounds and clap a simple rhythm after it has been demonstrated. The child should also be able to concentrate for a reasonable length of time, which is quite a strain for many small children. Perhaps the biggest indication that a child is ready to read is his motivation – if he enjoys listening to stories and actually expresses a desire to read. Often young children will point out their name or ask which word says the name of a character in a story, indicating that they are ready to begin.

The first preparations towards reading are those that many parents make naturally: reading stories aloud to their children and looking at picture books. The child should sit next to the parent while the parent is reading, so that he can see the words and pictures. If the parent runs a finger lightly under the words as she says them, the child will get used to the idea that those squiggles on the page represent the words the parent is saying. Small simple books with a picture and a short caption on each page are ideal. The pictures should be interesting and the print large, clear and well spaced. The parent should talk about the picture with the child and point to the words, explaining what the words say. Even when reading longer stories, the child may ask for certain words to be pointed out and even recognise them later.

The first principle is for the child to grasp the notion that words are shapes used to describe things. Often a child's own name is one of the first words he recognises and it is a good idea to have this prominently displayed somewhere, such as on the child's cabin door or over his bunk. It is very important to put into words experiences that a child has and so draw attention to the written word, for example: 'This is your book, it has your name on the cover,' or when watching a seabird, 'Shall we look in the bird book and find out that bird's name?' even if the parent knows very well what kind of bird it is. Such examples, although maybe seeming rather contrived to a parent, do help a child to realise what words are and their purpose. Many children have begun to learn to read at a parent's knee in this fashion. Once a child is interested and appears able to recognise some words in picture books, it is time to move on to a more definite scheme.

What is reading?

Before looking at different methods and reading schemes, it might be worthwhile to consider what reading is actually all about. It is the ability to recognise letter symbols, the way they are grouped together as words, and to decipher these in a left to right direction from the top to the bottom of the page. There are various ways in which a reader identifies words. Most common words are identified by their shape and features. These are recognised almost automatically, for most adults have long ago learnt and memorised them. In fact, when we adults read something new we tend to not even take in the common words; our eye only picks out major words or anything new or unusual. Children have to acquire this skill and commit common words to memory. This is the basis of the 'whole word' approach to learning to read and is excellent in the early stages. The limitation is that the English language has far too many words to be memorised and so the child must progress to other means of word identification.

A second way to identify unknown words is by the sound-symbol relationship, learning what sounds the letters and their combinations make and the rules and exceptions governing these. This is the basis of the 'phonic' method.

Thirdly, words can be identified by the structure of the sentence. Most children will not attempt to put a verb where the structure calls for a noun and vice versa. They know that 'this' is likely to be followed by 'is' and that 'I' is often followed by 'am'. In a similar way words are deduced from their context, the child putting in the word from his spoken language that makes the most sense. This informed guessing is the way that children teach themselves to improve their reading. For example, 'John beat out a .... on the drum' might produce the guess of 'rhythm', a difficult word when met in print for the first time.

An effective reader will use all these skills when faced with an unknown word and children should be encouraged to do so when learning to read.

Methods

The two main methods of teaching reading are the whole word approach, also called 'look and say', and the phonic method, where the child learns that letters stand for sounds.

In the whole word method, the child is taught to memorise whole words from the pattern and features of the word. This is the easiest and most natural method, especially for an infant. Among the words learnt at the beginning are commonly used words, such as the twelve words (a, of, and, that, he, the, I, was, to, in, is, it) which have been shown to make up on average one quarter of all reading matter. It has also been calculated that about one hundred common or key words make up half of the words used in everyday books and newspapers. Normally these basic words are learnt at an early stage along with the other words that make up the starting vocabulary of the first book in the reading scheme.

When a child tackles his first reading book he has a large chance of success if he already knows these words. The whole word method has the advantage of not restricting the vocabulary to simple words that follow the rules, so that more complicated words, such as 'aeroplane', can be introduced early on to make the stories the child reads more interesting. Even so, some of the schemes using this method have fallen into the trap of a meaningless and boring text, for although these key words are often repeated, they are in fact mainly linking words of little interest to a child.

The phonic approach, where words are sounded out, also produces some very boring and dull books, such as the 'cat sat on the mat' type. Most children are able to recognise whole words before they are ready for phonic techniques, so the phonic method is used mainly with older children.

The general consensus of opinion among teachers today is that a combination of methods should be used, commencing with the whole word method and progressing to phonic work when the child has a reasonable sight vocabulary. I would advise any parent against attempting to use any of the more unusual methods available, such as Pitman's Initial Teaching Alphabet (ita) or Gattegno's colour scheme for decoding words. Neither would there be much advantage in any of the reading laboratories and kits that claim to be scientific ways of teaching reading. These are little more than ordinary exercises in comprehension and phonics in a fancy package, and will not do the teaching for you.

Reading schemes

It is not necessary to use a commercially produced reading scheme at all, but the schemes do provide a structure and framework for the parent to work in, making it easier for her to see that the child is acquiring a good core vocabulary of key words. There are many reading schemes available, so what factors should guide one's choice? Firstly, choose one which uses attractive books with good stories and pictures, one that is likely to appeal to the particular child. Preferably the books should be short, for a child gets a great feeling of achievement from finishing a book and progressing to another. The sentences should be short, clearly written and with a good ratio of pictures to text. There should be a small starting vocabulary and the very gradual introduction of new words. While frequent repetition of words is necessary, the language should not be too stilted and false. Also look to see that the gradient from one book to the next is not too steep – that is, new words should not be introduced too fast after the first books. Another aspect that might influence one, is whether there are workbooks to accompany the series and a teacher's manual or guide.

It is not easy to recommend a particular scheme, although the Ladybird Key Words Reading Scheme is widely available in many countries, relatively inexpensive and has accompanying workbooks. There are three books with the same vocabulary at each level and the first levels are well graded, introducing most of the key words. The storyline is not very exceptional, but there is a handbook, *Teaching Reading*, and notes for using the scheme. Ladybird also produce *Puddle Lane* by Sheila McCullagh, a reading programme specifically aimed at parents helping their children to read. These stories have the text for the parent to read aloud to the child on the left-hand side and simple words for the child to read below the picture on the right-hand side of the page.

The *Pirate Readers*, also by Sheila McCullagh, were great favourites of my children, mainly because the stories are well written, interesting and have a nautical flavour. They were originally intended for older children who were slow in learning, but their story interest makes them suitable for younger children living afloat. The series also has accompanying workbooks and teaching material. Sheila McCullagh is one of the finest writers of reading schemes, and *One, Two, Three and Away* is another series written by her which has an interesting content and is especially suitable for the young beginner.

A scheme in common use in American schools is the Houghton Mifflin Reading Program. This scheme is very attractively illustrated in bright colours with clear print and a variety of different stories instead of one storyline. The first few books in the scheme are short, but the rest are rather bulky, containing many shorter stories, poems, factual topics and things to do. After every few stories is a skill lesson, which explores other language skills, such as how to use paragraphs or words of more than one meaning. The early books in this scheme might need some supplementing at the same level before moving on.

Look and say

The first step is to help the child learn the basic words that he will meet in the first book of the scheme. The words can be printed in clear lower-case (not capital) letters on cards about the size of business cards. The child looks at these 'flashcards' while the parent says the word, then the card is turned over so the word is hidden. Later the card is turned back and the child is asked what the word says. The cards can be shuffled about, introduced in a different order and played with as a game, asking the child to pick out a particular word from four or five cards and later from the whole selection. Anything that uses these first words, such as writing captions under the child's own drawing, will be an aid to his reading.

When the first words have been learnt the child can start to read the first book in the scheme out aloud, page by page. This stage should not be rushed and the child should not be asked to read longer than his concentration and interest span, any mistakes being corrected gently. If the child cannot concentrate for too long, it is better to break up the reading time into shorter, more frequent periods. This flexibility is an advantage the parent has over schools and set lessons. It cannot

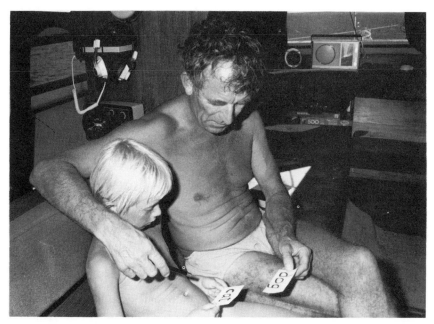

John Whitmore using flashcards to teach Sam to read.

be emphasised enough how important it is for a child to achieve success with this very first reading book, so do not try to introduce it before all the words are learnt. Patience is the key note here. It has been shown that even the brightest of children may need around twenty repetitions of a word before it is committed to the long-term memory, especially for the less interesting words. This is the reason why words are repeated several times in reading books after they have been first introduced.

When the first book has been read, it is wise to progress to a parallel reader, if the scheme has parallel books, before progressing to the next level. This consolidates what has been learnt. Similarly if the child wishes to reread a book, this is also to be encouraged as a consolidation of words learnt, especially if several mistakes were made. This should be done in the spirit of 'That book was fun to read, shall we read it again?' not 'Let's read it again because you made mistakes.'

The teacher's guide to a scheme will often give ideas for other activities to be carried out in parallel, and this is where workbooks printed especially for the scheme are useful. One activity which greatly aids reading is for the child to compose a short sentence about a picture that he has drawn, perhaps being encouraged to draw a picture based on the story he has read. The adult then writes this sentence under the picture in large, clear, well-spaced words, again in lower-case print-style letters. The child can trace over these words or try to copy them, then read them out. This activity assists reading not only by the reading out of the words, but by making the child aware of the shape and structure of words. Writing is a positive aid to word recognition and memorisation. Because the child is providing his own reading material from personal experience, it usually holds a great interest for him and puts meaning into the activity of reading. The more repetition that goes into the captions under the drawings the better, and the parent can guide the choice of words to some extent.

Once a child has started reading, the parent should still carry on reading stories aloud to the him, tracing along the lines with her finger. Children love to be retold their favourite stories and often will attempt to read books of nursery rhymes and other stories that they know well. Because they are familiar and well known, the child can read them more easily, often absorbing any new words with little difficulty.

For the beginner, the parent should thoroughly prepare a story or any material that the child is going to read. The book can be read aloud beforehand by the parent, which is always a good check that it is not too boring or difficult for the level of the child's reading. If the child knows the story, he can then concentrate his effort on deciphering the words, making intelligent guesses at any new words from the context. This should not be regarded as cheating, for anything that helps a child achieve fluency and comprehension in his reading is valid. The end result is what matters, not the way it was reached.

Resist the temptation to overteach, but rather use the principle of patient guidance, letting the child correct his own mistakes if possible or predict new words. If a child stops at a word or reads it wrong, he is often able to deduce his mistake or what the unknown word should be by reading further on in the sentence. Guidance throughout should be gentle in prompting new words and correcting mistakes.

Rereading books that a child has enjoyed should be encouraged, for this will help him gain in confidence and speed. If the first time the child guessed ten per cent of the words from the context, it is highly likely that he will recognise more and reduce this to five per cent on the second reading. That all important repetition is thus achieved in an enjoyable way. Basically the tenet is that reading is learned only by reading and more reading.

When a child has made a start at reading, supplementary readers, such as the excellent Dr Seuss and P.D. Eastman books, are highly recommended. Another activity to promote reading is to tape a favourite story from the text, but leaving out words here and there. The child follows the written version while listening to the tape and tries to fit the missing words into the story.

Phonics

As the child progresses he will probably start to work out some of the other clues to identifying new words, such as using the initial letter of a word. At this point he is probably ready for some phonic work. A child cannot start this kind of work until he can distinguish the separate sounds that make a word. He must also understand that each word has its own sound pattern which can be broken down into separate sounds, and that these sounds correspond to letter shapes or combinations of letter shapes, which are arranged in a definite sequence.

Typical questions to see if a child is ready for phonics would be:

'Which of the following words has a different sound at the beginning?'
    ship,   shoe,   dog,   shop
'Which of the following words has a different ending to the others?'
    ring,   sing,   sun,   wing

The simplest work in phonics can begin with the child drawing pictures of objects beginning with the same sound, starting with easier consonants and leaving the vowels and consonants such as q x y z j until later. The sounds that letters make are more important than the alphabetical names. Using both alphabetical and sound names can confuse some children, so the alphabet is better learnt at another time, separately from the phonic work.

From the initial letters one can progress to ending letters and common syllables, such as 'ing' or 'ed' and the plural 's'. Words that rhyme can be joined together as a game with lines of different colours.

cat   ring   play   boat   shop
top   goat   sing   bat   way

The next stage is to introduce common digraphs, such as ch, th, sh and wh. At this point the child should be taught to blend simple combinations of vowels and consonants into words, such as b-a-t as bat and d-o-g as dog.

These simple correspondences of letters and sounds are quite easy to explain, but no one can hope to teach all the rules and exceptions in the English language for there are hundreds of them. A lot of the most commonly used words are exceptions to rules, which is why they have to be memorised early. Fortunately children absorb a lot of these rules and exceptions during their reading in an unconscious manner. Some rules, however, are easy to explain and worth introducing early to aid progress, such as the silent e rule. This is often explained as a magic e which makes a vowel sound its alphabetical name and not its phonetic sound. For example:

hat – hate
rid – ride

Other work can be done in phonics to point out the sounds of common vowel combinations such as oo, ee, ea, ai and diphthongs such as ow, aw, ou, oi. The way that consonants blend together at the beginning of words can also be worked on: sounds such as st and sp, dr, gr, pl, bl, etc. This is a short step to the blends that occur at the ends of words, such as nd, nt, ck, mp, rt, etc. In sounding out new words the child should always be encouraged to use and blend syllables rather than sound out letter by letter, so that caterpillar should be broken down into cat-er-pill-ar not the drawn out and nonsensical c-a-t-e-r-p-i-l-l-a-r.

All this phonic work can be carried out alongside other reading practice and the learning of whole words by heart. One of the simplest ways is to have a small exercise book with a page for each new sound. Discuss with the child which words he can think of with the particular sound in it, at the beginning, end or middle of the word. A list of this sound family can then be written in the book:

all – tall, fall, small, wall

st – stop, stamp, station, street

The child can copy the words and underline the sound combination in colour, also drawing a small picture to illustrate the word where this is possible, as a memory aid. Later the list can be read out over again. This kind of phonic work overlaps with the beginnings of writing and spelling.

These exercises should never become too boring and repetitive, nor be dwelt on for too long if it is obvious that a child has mastered the sound and how letters represent it. Once a child has grasped some blends and rules, he will often work out for himself other similar combinations. Phonic work can easily be presented as fun, from I-spy games to finding the odd sound out, the kind of activity most children enjoy. There are many commercially produced games and workbooks that can be used in this context, such as the *English Work Books* by Ronald Ridout. Another excellent book is *Word Games for the Teaching of Reading* by Nicolson and Williams. These two Australian teachers are specialists in helping children with difficulties, but the many games outlined in this book provide ideas to make learning reading skills less boring for any child.

All the time the child will be reading more and more, so that any difficulty he has with particular letters or sounds can be given attention as soon as they are noticed. Common confusions occur between the tailed letters y, g, p and q, and similarly children often confuse the two reverse pairs b and d, p and q. A parent alert to this can give plenty of practice to prevent the confusion.

More and more books

There are many stages in reading as the child climbs step by step up the ladder towards automatic word recognition. As well as learning sound combinations and phonic rules, one important aspect is the understanding and comprehension of the text. It is most important that a child is motivated to read and should do so for pleasure. Once a child has started reading, do encourage him to read as much as possible, but be careful to keep the reading matter within his capability. In the early stages, when a child may spend a long time identifying individual words, a selection of interesting books at his level will help to sustain him in his efforts. If the reading matter is too difficult he may be discouraged and lose sight of the purpose in reading. Providing enough good reading material is one of the headaches of teaching afloat, not only because of the weight and space problem but also the expense. One cannot possibly carry the range and variety that a good school would have to offer. If one spends some time in a port, it might be

Many sailing children soon become avid readers, their skills improved by more and more reading.

149

possible to borrow books from a public library. Fortunately quite a lot of good books are published in cheaper editions that are not too bulky.

By choosing books carefully, one can direct a child towards 'good' books that will develop not only his language, but also his imagination. Well-written books by both classic and modern authors can usually be read and reread at different levels, a great advantage for a boat's limited library. For young readers, simple adaptations of legends and fairy tales are always popular, or folk tales such as the adventures of Robin Hood. Animal stories are another favourite, such as Michael Bond's series on Paddington Bear, or characters such as the imaginary Moomin family adventures by Tove Jansson. Non-fiction should not be neglected either, as simple factual books often appeal to a more mechanically minded child. At the beginner's level these are more difficult to find, although Macdonald Starters and Ladybird both have a reasonable selection, books on the sea and boats being popular with sailing children.

The classics should not be introduced too early because these do require a certain reading standard, but around nine or ten years old a child could be given such books as *Alice in Wonderland, Treasure Island, Tom Sawyer* or *Black Beauty*. The books of many modern writers such as C.S. Lewis (the *Narnia* books), Roald Dahl, Alan Garner and Richard Adams, to name but a few, are fast on the way to becoming classics of children's literature. The writer who appears to have a place on every cruising boat with children on board is Arthur Ransome. The many books in his *Swallows and Amazons* series are swapped back and forth, wherever sailing children gather. Trading books between boats is the standard way to renew one's floating library and one of the ways sailing children make new friends. Choosing books that are enjoyed and loved is essential when space is limited, for they will probably have to be reread many times.

If possible one should listen to a child read every day, even if only one page, and certainly listen to every page of a set reading scheme book. As the child becomes more fluent, this can become less frequent – say, every three days for the average eight year old and once a week at ten or eleven. This is necessary to observe progress and note any difficulties. It provides an opportunity to discuss new words and check by asking questions that the child understands what he is reading. It is also a way of checking that the child is not trying to read books that are too difficult for him.

Language experience

There is another approach to reading called the 'language experience method' which, although limited as a single method, is a valuable addition alongside other reading programmes. This is a development from the writing of captions under drawings and involves the child in making his own books to read from.

The child makes up or tells his own story, which the parent jots down or records on tape. Then the story is written out by the parent in clear print-style words into a story book, preferably one with some space left for the child to illustrate the story. The story can be read back to the child and then he can read it on his own. Children often get great pleasure out of reading their own stories, before they have the dexterity to write them themselves, as beginners usually write very slowly and cannot get their thoughts down fast enough. This is also a method for stimulating creative writing. The limitation of this approach is that it does not bring about any growth in the child's vocabulary nor develop his language, and new words and expressions are essential to reading progress.

Reading growth

Now we come to the question of tackling growth and development in the child who is already reading quite well. Children often make progress in spurts, making seemingly little progress for a while and then taking a big leap forward. This sometimes comes with a phonic breakthrough when they suddenly understand a rule. In the seemingly fallow period when little progress appears to be made, the child might well be consolidating his previous learning. Often children will choose to read for pleasure slightly below their attainment level, for in this way they enjoy the story without the strain of dealing with too many unknown words. This tendency will also occur if the child is ill or seasick. My own children used to read easier material when the weather was rough and on longer ocean passages.

One of the advantages of teaching a child in a one-to-one relationship is that reading skills can be pursued further than normally happens in school, where the teacher may tend to concentrate on the slower pupils and not have time for those reading reasonably well. One of the most important aspects is to develop understanding and comprehension of the reading material. This can be done by asking questions and encouraging the use of a dictionary.

Phonic work can be extended to more difficult groupings, such as words ending in -ious or -ation and to silent letters such as k or g. This language development can involve word study in a variety of ways; for example, making lists of words pronounced the same but spelt differently, words with multiple meanings, or synonyms and antonyms. It might involve making lists of new words and their meanings, or looking at how words are derived with prefixes and suffixes. All of this kind of work has an obvious overlap with writing and spelling, being part and parcel of the child's whole language development. An excellent series of books which studies words in this way from the simplest level to a very advanced standard is the *Word Perfect* series by Ronald Ridout.

Older children can also be taught specific reading techniques; for example, skimming to read something quickly such as a notice or a newspaper article, or scanning to find some particular information. Further growth in reading involves increasing the speed of reading while still retaining full comprehension, as opposed to the skimming technique. For this the child must break any habit of lip movements or pointing to words, for these inhibit the eye moving along the line more quickly. Speed is increased by regular reading of material below the child's level, which also boosts confidence.

How, then, can one tell how a child is progressing? There are various reading tests, which usually give a score as a reading age to be compared with the child's chronological age, but these tests have limitations and are only a rough guide. The commonest ones in use are the Schonell Graded Word Reading Test in Britain and the Gates and MacGinitie Reading Tests in the United States. In Schonell's test, single isolated words are grouped in rows of five and the child is asked to read them one by one. Success or failure is noted on another paper and when ten errors have been made the test is stopped. From the number of words read correctly, the child's reading age is calculated. If it is decided to use a test, the instructions should be followed very carefully, never teaching the words in the test nor helping the child by prompting as this makes the test worthless. There is no value in testing frequently; once a year is sufficient, and not too much store should be set by the result. It is probably better to assess your child by listening carefully to him read, noting in your records the reading scheme books he has read correctly, the type of mistakes he makes and any special problems.

Reading problems

Problems and difficulties encountered in reading can be due to a variety of reasons, but are less likely to persist in the parent teaching situation than in the classroom, because the particular difficulty is usually spotted and help given earlier. Varying amounts of difficulty will be experienced by children of lower ability or with any defects of sight, speech or hearing. For any suspected defect, expert advice should be sought, as the wearing of glasses to correct a sight defect can bring about speedy results. This is especially true of minor defects, which often are not noticed until a child begins to read. If a child has a hearing disability so that he cannot distinguish well between different sounds, he should practise listening to and repeating sounds that are similar, such as b and p.

Some children experience difficulty in reading because of emotional disturbances, and this can be one result of pushing too hard and too early. Other children are just late developers and will often catch everyone by surprise by making up time later on in one big spurt. With the slow reader it is essential to be patient, not hurrying him and providing lots of interesting material within his grasp.

If a child tends to misread words frequently and has trouble recognising individual words, he will need a lot more practice looking at word shapes. Again this can be achieved as a form of play activity and with games. For these children new words should be introduced very slowly and lots of practice given at the same level, with supplementary books before moving to the next level.

Particular problems may crop up, such as substituting one letter for another, omitting or adding letters and words, mispronunciation and the reversal of letters and words. These problems can be dealt with as they occur by relevant exercises similar to those outlined in the phonic work section. One of the commonest mistakes among beginners is that they are unable to distinguish between a shape and its mirror image, such as b and d, or n and u. The group of letters, b, d, g, p and q are also easily confused, especially when the child does not have the left to right skill and cannot distinguish between inverted objects or reads 'saw' as 'was', for example. These mistakes are very common but do not appear to prevent reading progress in most children and usually gradually disappear, again aided by solid phonic work.

Left to right orientation and training left to right eye movements is important and some physical factors such as mixed-handedness and -eyeness do appear to have an effect on reading ability. As a child matures, one hemisphere in the brain becomes dominant; for a right-handed right-eyed person the left side of the brain is dominant, while the right side is dominant for a left-hander with a master left eye. In some children this dominance is late in establishing itself and they also might have crossed laterality, being right-handed and left-eyed or vice versa. These children have a greater tendency to make the errors of inversion and reversion. Establishing a definite side in a child, whether it is the right or the left, may help in this matter, but the problem often resolves itself as the child matures.

The term 'dyslexia' has become popular as a blanket term for the real unexplained reading difficulties that some children have. Many reasons have been put forward why some children, who are often quite able in other fields such as mathematics, do not make progress in reading. The confusion between left and right might well be one factor contributing to this, as might the lack of an established cerebral dominance. Hyperactivity is another reason sometimes given to explain these reading difficulties. For each child, different factors might contribute, so an individual assessment is necessary. Obviously if one suspects that a child has a serious reading problem, professional advice should be sought; it is well beyond the scope of this book.

In this chapter I have tried to outline some of the basic ideas involved in learning to read in order to help the parent who is tackling the task of teaching a child, either from the beginning or extending and improving the skills of a child already reading. Finally I would like to emphasise that nothing improves reading quicker

153

than reading, and most sailing children do become avid readers. Parents can help a child achieve this in many ways, from listening to him read, to encouraging his reading techniques and providing him with enjoyable reading material. Reading well and for pleasure is an achievement to be proud of for both child and parent alike.

Books

Houghton Mifflin Reading Program. (1982) Boston, Massachusetts: Houghton Mifflin Co.

Moyle, D. (1968) *The Teaching of Reading.* London: Ward-Lock Educational.

Murray, W. (1979) *Ladybird Key Words Reading Scheme.* Loughborough: Ladybird Books Ltd.

McCullagh, S. (1985) *Puddle Lane.* Loughborough: Ladybird Books Ltd.

McCullagh, S. (1959) *Pirate Readers.* London: E. J. Arnold & Sons Ltd.

McCullagh, S. (1981) *One, Two, Three and Away.* London: Collins Educational.

Nicholson, D. and Williams, G. (1975) *Word Games for the Teaching of Reading.* London: Pitman Publishing.

Ridout, R. (1978) *English Work Books.* London: Ginn & Co.

Ridout, R. (1960) *Word Perfect.*

Thompson, B. (1979) *Reading Success: a guide for parents and teachers.* London: Sidgwick & Jackson.

14
Language Development

Language is probably the supreme achievement of man, that which distinguishes us from other animals. Through language we communicate our thoughts to others and through language we share the experiences of others. It is the medium through which we draw upon our written history and so inherit our culture. The development of language in all its modes, whether talking, listening, reading or writing, is thus central to any child's development. In younger children all these aspects are taught together, the spoken vocabulary being developed while the child learns to read and write. Even in older children, the language skills are still entwined and related one to another. The important skill of reading has been dealt with separately in another chapter, so here I wish to concentrate on writing, although many of the aspects considered in the teaching of reading will have a great effect on writing as well, particularly spelling.

As has been pointed out earlier, children pass through a series of developmental stages in their thinking and this affects their spoken language. Young children do think differently to adults and this is reflected in their speech. This is best seen in the monologue that a young child will keep up while playing, talking aloud to no one in particular. In order to develop social speech and to be able to carry on a meaningful conversation, a child will need a lot of practice in talking.

Talking and listening will therefore take a prime place in a child's development as he begins to learn to read and write. The young child should be encouraged to express himself in words and the parent should listen carefully to what he has to say, resisting the tendency to 'talk at' the child without listening

Children who are cruising have plenty to say. Talking, as well as writing, plays an important part in language development.

to his point of view. It is pointless to expect children to express themselves in writing if they have no experience in expressing themselves orally. This can be incorporated into the education programme by encouraging the child to talk about something that happened or to verbalise what he has been doing or playing with. Learning to recite nursery rhymes and sing simple songs aids a child's speech, and this can be expanded into asking him to retell a favourite story in his own words.

Even with older children, talking and listening should not be neglected. Instead of writing, sometimes they can talk about a particular subject, possibly recording their talk on a tape recorder. Writing can be very laborious, especially in the early stages, and often children's thoughts race faster than they can write them down. Telling a story instead of writing it can sometimes relieve this frustration and liberate a child from concentrating too much on the mechanics of forming letters with a pencil.

Children need practice in speaking, but this is one item that most children living afloat seem to get plenty of. Not only are they living in a stimulating environment, but it is very much an adult world. Most cruising children are used to talking to adults, apart from their immediate family, which is probably the reason why all the cruising children I have spoken to have impressed me by the fluent manner in which they express themselves.

156

Handwriting

The spoken word leads to the written word, yet the hardest language skill that a child has to master is that of writing. A good coordination between hand and eye is needed and a fine control over smaller movements of the hand, one which many younger children do not possess. The achievement of this fine control can be helped in many ways during a young child's normal play – building with bricks and other construction toys, throwing and catching a ball, making shapes out of plasticine and cutting out with scissors (under supervision). The best preparation for writing, however, is drawing and colouring. A child should be guided from the beginning to hold pencils correctly between the thumb and first two fingers. A decent length and size of pencil should always be used for a young child, not one that is too small or thin.

The first step towards writing can be tracing over and then copying words that the parent has written. The child's own name is an obvious first choice, as all children are very highly motivated and get great pleasure out of being able to write their own name. Simple captions to their drawings and pictures can also be traced or copied. Practice in drawing shapes, circles and straight lines, both vertical and horizontal, will help in the formation of letters. These shapes can be practised in the form of patterns, such as:

Letters for a child to trace or copy should be large and bold, about one centimetre (half an inch) high and in lower-case print, not capitals. This print style uses the type of letters that will be met with first in books, while capital letters can easily be taught later on.

Writing should begin on plain paper first, as most children start by writing very large and lines on the page can inhibit them. Quite soon, however, they can progress to paper with widely spaced lines to help keep their writing straight and of even size. Another useful aid in the beginning is to outline letters with dots for the child to join with a continuous line, a halfway stage between tracing and copying. This method is commonly used in workbooks, which are a good buy for the teaching of handwriting.

The letters are usually introduced in groups of those with similar hand movements, such as anticlockwise or linear, for there is no advantage in introducing them in alphabetical order. A suitable order to introduce the letters would be:

t i j k l z f	– all are line letters and go from top to bottom
a c d e g o q	– all have an anticlockwise movement
b p	– the two letters that are written clockwise
h m n r	– these are sometimes called the 'hump' letters
u v w y	– these are the 'trough' letters
x and s	– do not fit into any group

Practising writing letters is slow and laborious, so it is better to have very short sessions more often – say, every day writing one letter just six times. As writing without a purpose appears futile to a child, do not rely too heavily on exercises but intersperse the practise of individual letters with other writing such as simple phrases to caption drawings. As writing is so much more laborious and harder than reading, some teachers feel that children cannot be expected to write freely until they can read about a hundred words. They will, however, progress towards this freer writing, firstly with single words, then phrases and finally sentences.

At the beginning children need a lot of help and guidance in forming the letters, and one should deal gently with any mistakes in the writing of their first words, such as poor spacing or spelling. The child can be guided in several ways towards the correct proportioning of letters and spacing between words. The width of the little finger is a rough guide to the space between words, while the tall letters can be explained as being, with their 'tails' or 'tops', about twice the size of the small letters.

Only when a degree of fluency in writing the lower-case letters has been mastered should the capitals be practised. Again these can be given in groups. Firstly, the capital letters made with a single stroke, namely C I L O S U V W; these can be followed by B D G J M P Q R T X Y which need two strokes of a pencil, and finally by A E F H K N which are made with three or four strokes. Once the capital letters have been taught, the child can be shown where they are used, at the beginning of every sentence and for the names of people. It is also a logical moment to introduce the full stop.

A parent would probably be well advised to purchase one of the series of workbooks that deal with handwriting practice. In these there are often patterns to copy as a step in the direction of joined-up or cursive writing. Around eight years old the child can begin practising loops and joined patterns, gradually progressing to learning how to join letters to others using 'tails' at the beginning and end of each letter. The particular style of writing chosen, whether cursive, italic or Marion Richardson type, will depend much on personal preference, the simplest style probably being the easiest to teach on a moving boat. Whichever style is taught, however, the aim should be for clarity, legibility and ease of flow. Joining letters should not be attempted until print script has been mastered.

Creativity and content

Children in the initial stages of learning to write are so absorbed in the actual writing process that it is a lot to expect of them to be also creative. The word 'creative' itself has been rather misused as regards children's writing, as though the right kind of stimulation and teaching will automatically produce literary writing of the highest order. In fact, anything that is genuine self-expression can be regarded as 'creative', whether this is an imaginative story or a factual account of a scientific observation. Children vary so much in their tastes as well as in their talents that one must beware of trying to force the budding scientist into trying unsuccessfully to be a potential winner of a prize for fiction. That does not mean that he should not be able to write a clear factual account of his scientific work. Our aim should be to develop in children the ability to write effectively for the various requirements that they will meet in adult life, and also to make them alive to the potential of language as a means of self-expression. If this can stimulate them into such activities as writing poetically, all well and good; but one should not be too fanatical about it.

The kind of standard to be aimed at by the time a child has reached about eleven years old and is embarking on the secondary level of education would include the ability to make up an interesting story, to write a clear letter, to write a review or appreciation of a book he has read and to be able to write clearly about a factual event or experience, such as a scientific experiment or an excursion ashore.

Beginning writing

As mentioned earlier, when a reading ability of about a hundred words has been attained and the child has the ability to form letters, he can be encouraged to write in his own words brief sentences or phrases about something that interests him or that he has done. The age at which this occurs will vary from child to child, although normally it will be between five and seven years of age. At this stage the child should not be asked to write too much and will need a lot of help. Children like to start writing in a clean new book, so to keep this stimulation it is better to use quite small books and to begin each piece of writing on a new page.

These young children are often inhibited in their writing by the fact that their handwriting is slow and by their inability to spell words. The whole process of transferring speech and thoughts onto paper can be quite daunting, so the child will need positive encouragement and congratulation on every part of his writing that is effective, such as a good description.

Talking with the child beforehand about what he is going to write is particularly helpful and any key words he needs can be written on a card or in a book – maybe words such as rocket, engine, spaceship, to use in a description under a drawing of a spaceship. By asking the child about his drawing or the subject he is going to write about, the parent can try to draw out descriptive words and expand the child's sentences. For example, a child might want to write about a house he has constructed out of Lego. A fuller description of this house can be elicited by asking questions as to whether the house is big or small, what colours the bricks are, if it has doors, windows, a roof, etc. A small book can be started as a personal dictionary with a page for each letter of the alphabet. The parent writes on the appropriate page the correct spelling of whatever word the child requires. This can then be referred back to on other occasions, and will also develop a sense of alphabetical order for dictionary use later on.

Much of a child's early writing will centre around everyday events and take the form of a simple diary. It is too much to ask a small child to write about things that happened some time ago or are more complex. Usually this writing will quickly develop into longer accounts, which are often ungrammatical and lacking punctuation, the word 'and' typically being used with great frequency as a form of punctuation. This does not matter very much at this stage; the important thing is to get the words and writing flowing. A typical piece of writing from a beginner is this from my son Ivan at the age of five:

> to day we were looking for a beach and we found a beach and we anchored at the beach. we went for a swim and daddy went snorkelling

A year later at six he could write:

> on the twenty secend of april we went to pompeii it was covered with ash and lava from the volcano vesuvius. first we went to the basilica. after that we went to the forum too there I gave mary a fright. then we went to the main road. there we saw in the middle of the road steping stones. there are steping stones across there because of the rubbish. we walked down the main road then we turned of to the theatre the theatre was oval shaped and most of the steps and seats are missing. the grass has grown in the places were the missing steps and seats are. then we went to see the volcano that covered pompeii. it is still alive today. At the museum we saw some of the things that were in the houses of pompei. the things that i liked best were two deers. the deers were statues. there were some other statues of ladies that danced round the Roman baths. then we went to see lots of mosaics. they were made of tiny tiny stones. there was a mosaic that looked like a picture from far away.

So as not to spoil the flow and fluency, do not cover the work with too much red pencil. Words wrongly spelt can be pointed out and practised later, while any grammar or punctuation can be worked on in a separate language book. In the piece quoted above, Ivan could have been encouraged to begin his sentences with capital letters or do work on how some letters get doubled when a suffix like

-ing is added, e.g. step – stepping. This could be followed up by making a list of other examples, such as stop – stopping, run – running. Language work that is done close in time to particular mistakes is always more relevant and more likely to be corrected in future work.

To encourage the flow of writing, use can be made of a tape recorder for stories, or the parent can jot down the child's words and later write them into a story book, as described in the reading chapter. Another way of encouraging writing is to ask the child to write in his own words a familiar story that has been read to him. This relieves the child from the pressure of having to devise his own story from scratch. Alternatively the child can be shown a picture and asked to write a story about it.

It is quite difficult for a child to select his own subject and the directive 'write a story' with no help whatsoever is asking rather a lot. The parent should choose a topic and provide some stimulation to start the child thinking. It is always better to begin with the child and his experiences, and fortunately plenty of interesting things do happen in the world of cruising that can provide a starting point. The child could be asked to describe the moods or colours of the sea or what a storm was like, a place visited ashore or something found on a beach. The starting point can be quite simple and does not have to be fictional.

Only once a child can write several sentences is it possible to progress to made-up stories. This will need more help than writing about personal experiences and an adult can suggest an idea – even if from the perennial favourites of animals, ghosts or princesses. One can move from a story that has been read aloud to talk about similar ideas and provide words that could be used in the story. Building a house on a deserted island, shipwrecks, pirates and monster stories are favourite topics for young shipboard children.

Reading different stories or poems and talking about different topics will enable one to find out what appeals to a particular child. Often children write very little because they find a subject dull. What inspires one child will not inspire another, so one has to use some judgement. It is often better to choose small themes rather than large ones. If a child becomes involved in a too complicated and ambitious story, he is likely to get frustrated and be unable to finish. Better to write a story about a boat trip around a lagoon than fail to write a story about a voyage around the world.

Ideas for writing about

Animals. This can include imaginary or fantasy animals from dragons to unicorns, or extinct animals such as dinosaurs. Another topic could be a real animal a child has known, such as a cat or dog. Spiders, tigers or snakes can also catch the imagination and there are many stories and poems involving animals that can be read aloud. Aesop's fables are one such source of inspiration.

Alternatively, stories could be written about an elephant who does not forget or a dolphin who rescues a child.

Spooks. All the forms of ghosts, witches and supernatural beings are a good base for stories. Spells can be made up and the child encouraged to try and frighten the reader with his story.

Space. Another popular topic is outer space, which offers the possibility of spaceships, descriptions of other planets and extraterrestrial beings, or how it feels to walk in space. There is plenty of scope in this topic for the imagination to fly.

The sea. As a permanent presence in the environment, the sea should provide lots of ideas, from a storm at sea to a submarine journey or exploring a sunken wreck. The child can imagine he is a skin diver and can meet anything from a mermaid to a shark or monster of the depths. Most sailing children have little trouble in writing vivid stories involving shipwrecks, pirates, hurricanes or rescues at sea.

The senses. Children can be asked to write descriptive pieces after carefully using one or other of the senses: how things look or how they feel; imagining a place as it would be sensed by a blind man; the sounds of a particular place, whether it is a fairground, market or a windy day at sea. Favourite foods or meals can be described, or an advertisement for them written, or a particular taste described to a visitor from another planet. The special smells of places, from the galley to the fish harbour, can also be written about, while all the senses can be combined in descriptions of a busy market, a carnival, a fête or even the beach.

Ivan, when asked to write about the sounds that he could hear in the cockpit if he closed his eyes, wrote a simple laconic list:

> Aeroplane, bells, typewriter.
> Now and again cars,
> Wind in Baroness's rigging
> For a while Crista rowing
> Birds calling

On a similar occasion, twelve year old Doina, being two years older than Ivan, produced this:

> Tropical Sounds
>
> Green palm trees rustling
> in the wind;
> answering its restless
> whispering of unknown lands
> the noise is like a gentle hiss
> patient and uncomplaining.

The endless roar
of the infinite waves that ever
crash and break on a reef,
dying away with a sigh and a
splash
for always

The birds:
they chatter gossip
winging away through the wind
and sit on a branch quarrelling
scolding each other

The crickets too,
their chirping fills the cool night air
and all these sounds blending so
beautiful they become
the best orchestra on earth.

Writing poetry falls into a special category, and as a teacher it is very difficult to inspire, although reading a wide range of poetry does provide some stimulus. Children can often write in rhyme or make up limericks, but there is little justification in pressing a child to write poetry as a matter of routine. Of course if they show interest in expressing their feelings or thoughts in this way, they should be encouraged. Doina often wrote poems for herself from her own ideas outside of our school programme, as it is a medium she loves and enjoys, but my more scientifically minded son Ivan could never be persuaded in a poetic direction. This example illustrates how children vary both in their talents and interests, the advantage of personal teaching being that individual differences can be catered for.

A child's writing, whether prose or poetry, can be improved in many ways. Descriptive words can be discussed and encouraged; for example, if writing about the bark of a tree, one could bring in such words as rough, smooth, slippery, knobbly, knotted, gnarled, coarse, furrowed, etc. Similarly the use of well-worn words can be questioned. (What do you mean by it being a 'nice' day? Was it warm, sunny, blue-skied, beautiful, pleasant, enjoyable, pleasurable, amusing, quiet or bustling with activity?) Making lists of words to describe different things, such as things hot and things cold, is a typical example of a way to increase word power. Another example of how this can be made more interesting is to write all the words for what can be done with one's hands in a large outline traced around a hand, or all the things done with feet in an outline drawn around a foot.

The technique of jotting down words or thoughts in note form first can be suggested. It is sometimes helpful to write a rough draft, which is then discussed. After all, this is what adults usually do when they have to write something, and it is certainly how this book was written – ideas put down as notes, then a first draft followed by careful revision. We should not be so presumptuous as to expect children to trot out a perfect final draft. Also it can be inhibiting if a child thinks he can never alter something after it has been written. Children should always be encouraged to read their work through, even from the earliest age, for they often spot and correct their own errors that way.

A way of developing a sense of pride in work well done is to prepare a good copy of a piece of work for display on a bulkhead or in a special folder. Any spelling mistakes and errors can be corrected before it is rewritten. It can be time consuming to copy everything out a second time, so this should be reserved only for certain chosen pieces of work.

Imaginative writing is always expanded by reading, especially by reading what is called 'better' fiction. Discussing the books that children read and what they like or dislike about a book can also stimulate thought. Learning new words often comes out of reading, and this is very important in making writing more interesting as well. New words that a child comes across in his reading can be written down in a word book, although it is probably sufficient to discuss the meaning of a new word as the child tries to use it.

Writing falls into three basic categories: storytelling, which is both descriptive and imaginative; informative writing, such as recording facts and events; and evaluative writing, which involves commenting on events, books and the ideas of others. All three categories should be paid attention to, for writing cannot be regarded as a skill in isolation. Not only is writing closely allied to speech and reading, but it will also be used in all other subjects, particularly the informative and evaluative styles. Writing without a purpose sometimes can seem pointless to a child, so incorporating writing into definite projects, such as letters home to grandparents or friends, can provide practice with a purpose. However, some work will have to be done on spelling and grammar, but this is probably best accomplished separate from the actual creative writing.

Grammar and punctuation

Most educationalists agree that when a child starts to write one should go easy on the red pencil. But a parent may well ask at what point she should judge to intervene and when to leave alone. The techniques and rules of writing can be gradually suggested to the beginner, starting with explaining that sentences always begin with a capital letter and end with a full stop. The mistakes that children make in their writing are best followed up immediately they occur, by giving practice and explaining a particular rule. Once again, this immediate personal tuition is so much more relevant and productive than what is possible in a normal classroom. Many aspects of grammar will be absorbed naturally by the child during his reading. As a guide, the following list indicates roughly the order in which main points should be covered over a period of several years. Many of these points can be introduced at an appropriate moment in the child's writing progress.

(1) Sentences begin with a capital letter and end with a full stop.
(2) Capital letters are used for proper names, i.e. names of people, places, days, months.
(3) The use of the comma, which is best explained as a pause for breath, and also the question mark.
(4) How descriptive words called adjectives describe an object. The child can write different words to describe a particular noun, e.g. an old, brown, wooden, painted and cracked door.
(5) Similarly how adverbs add description to the verb, which can be explained as the action word in a sentence, e.g. writing down the different ways of running: slowly, quickly, swiftly, jerkily, etc.
(6) The proper use of joining words such as 'and', 'but', 'because', 'if'.
(7) The use of speech marks for what people say and the apostrophe for missing letters.
(8) How different tenses indicate past, present and future. A child can be asked to put sentences into different tenses.
(9) When to start a new paragraph and how this indicates a new line of thought.

Some books deal with the common difficulties of both grammar and spelling in novel ways and using word play. This kind of word study is contained in books such as *Word Perfect* by Ronald Ridout or the *Houghton Mifflin Reading Program*, both mentioned in the previous chapter. Other recommended books for language development are *Passwords* by Rose and Young and *Ideas* and *Young Ideas* by Edward Ramsbottom.

Spelling

There are two basic schools of thought about the teaching of spelling – one that spelling is something that is caught, the other that it should be taught. The 'caught' school developed out of a horror of boring spelling lists and insists on basing the work more on actual mistakes made by the child. Obviously this works better in a one-to-one situation than in a classroom. Most teachers agree that in the early stages of writing it can be inhibiting for a child if correct spelling is overemphasised. There is no quick and easy way to learn to spell correctly and some children find it much easier than others. It is a skill helped by lots of reading and practice in writing. The very common mistake of reversing the order of letters in words will usually diminish naturally as the child matures and should not be worried about in the beginning.

Even if not following a set scheme, I think some work on spelling does no harm, maybe commencing by learning the common words that children use frequently and often misspell. If a child can spell these often used words it also gives him confidence. This is the kind of schoolwork that can be done orally in small doses on passage or when the weather is not so good. The words can be put into groups such as 'what, when, where, which and who' or similarly spelt words such as 'night, fight, light', etc. This spelling work is interlinked with the phonic work outlined in the chapter on reading, and work on each of these aspects will reinforce the other.

For learning to spell more difficult words, the basic technique of look and cover, followed by writing down from memory, as outlined by Fitzgerald in his book *The Teaching of Spelling* is probably the most comprehensive method. His method can be summarised as comprising five stages.

(1) *Saying*. The child is shown the word, repeats it and then makes up a sentence with it orally.
(2) *Looking*. The child looks at the word, says it syllable by syllable, making an attempt to spell it.
(3) *Recalling*. The child closes his eyes and tries to spell the word out. This is repeated if he gets it wrong.
(4) *Writing*. The word is written from memory.
(5) *Mastering*. The word is written three times from memory. Any failure means a return to the beginning.

For lists of words for spelling practice, there are several small pamphlet-type books that can be purchased. Spelling differences between countries seem to present few problems for children, especially once a child can read and write reasonably well. Swapping books between various nationalities is quite commonplace among cruising children, and American children read English authors with ease and vice versa.

As I have pointed out before, all the language skills entwine, so that children will continually acquire knowledge of the basic roots and irregularities of spelling in their reading, word study and phonic work. Progress in any one of the language skills will automatically help the others. This will be augmented by writing connected with their other work, on such topics as history, geography and the sciences, which makes their writing more purposeful and will be explored in following chapters.

Books

Fitzgerald, J. A. (1951) *The Teaching of Spelling.* Milwaukee, Wisconsin: Bruce Books.

Ramsbottom, E. (1971) *Ideas and Young Ideas.* London: Macmillan.

Rose, J. and Young, P. (1978) *Passwords.* Edinburgh: Oliver & Boyd.

15
A Guide to Mathematics

In many respects learning to read and write has changed little over the years and there would be nothing amiss in parents teaching their children to read as they themselves were taught. In the realm of mathematics, however, there have been many sweeping changes, not only in methods but also in the content of what is taught in a modern school. The field of mathematics has expanded so much that children no longer spend time practising rows and rows of arithmetical examples, but are likely to be found exploring the beginnings of geometry or algebra at an early age, or manipulating binary numbers and matrices, dealing with concepts and relationships that their parents have maybe never heard of.

This 'new' or 'modern' mathematics has met with some opposition from those who felt that basic work in arithmetic, such as learning multiplication tables, was being neglected. As in every field the happy middle is probably the best path to take, compromising between the traditional and the progressive. Nevertheless the changes in mathematics cannot be ignored, because the society we live in has itself changed. Our children are growing up in a technological computerised age and should be educated so as to function effectively in it. Because of the widespread use of pocket calculators, many people see little point in children wasting time on complicated and lengthy computations. The important thing is that they understand the principles and concepts involved, and for this reason the early years and solid groundwork in basic mathematics have never been more important.

As explained in Chapter 9, all children's development has been shown to proceed in a definite sequence from the simple to the complex, and this applies to mathematical thought more than any other area of a child's development. Most commercially produced mathematics textbooks and workbooks follow the same logical sequence, and for this reason I would certainly recommend the use of such a series. This will ensure that topics are introduced in the right order and that all important mathematical ideas are adequately covered. It will also save a lot of time in devising mathematical problems and in working out the right answers. The continuity from the first book to later books in the same series may also be an advantage.

Choosing a series is always a matter of personal preference, and the attractiveness of the layout often influences this choice, especially as regards workbooks for the child to write his answers in. There is much to be said for using a series in common use in schools of one's country of origin, especially as regards the systems of measurement and money – the United States being one of the few countries that does not now use the metric system. Other points to look for are a teacher's manual or resource book to accompany the series, enrichment games or suggestions for supplementary activities. An answer book is absolutely essential! A bright child can whizz through some of the workbooks that require only simple figure answers, so it is important to check that the child does understand what he is doing. For this reason it might be worthwhile using more than one series to provide some diversity and consolidation at each level. Sometimes suggestions or problems given in a textbook are difficult to carry out on a boat, especially in respect of measuring and weighing activities. With some ingenuity, though, these can usually be adapted to the marine environment; for example, instead of a traffic survey, one could count the number of ketches, sloops and cutters in a marina when work is being done with simple statistics or when a graph has to be drawn.

In this chapter I am putting much more emphasis on the earlier rather than the later stages in mathematics. For older children I will only outline the basic topics that should be covered at different age levels by a correspondence course or mathematics book, as there is not space to give practical instructions for the whole field of mathematics. The ages given are only approximate as children do progress at different speeds, and with the personal tuition that sailing children get they may well move ahead with great speed.

Early years

The recommendation of a commercially produced series was intended particularly for older children and is not so vital, nor always possible, for the very young. The rudiments of mathematical thought can commence even before a child has learnt to count, and a child's early experiences form the basis for all later progress. Much of this experience will come through playing with such things as bricks, containers of different shapes and sizes, sand and water. All the time the child is amassing practical knowledge of the way in which the world is organised in respect of size, weight, colour, volume or time. This play lays down the foundations of mathematical understanding and by providing a rich variety of experiences parents can help a child to develop more rapidly.

Mathematics is based on three simple processes: sorting, matching and ordering. Practice in these three processes, from which all later mathematical work develops, can easily be provided for the young child.

'Sorting' or classification is fundamental to all logical thought, for to solve any problem one has to sort through the information available. Thus when deciding to make a particular ocean passage, the yachtsman has to consider routes, weather patterns, currents and seasons, sorting out which information is relevant to his needs. In the same way, a child will eventually have to be able to sort out the sounds that different letter combinations make when learning to read, or multiples of five to be able to tell the time easily.

For the young child sorting begins by arranging objects into groups or sets, whether it be bricks, buttons or shells. Asking a child to put all the red bricks into one pile is the simplest form of sorting. Sorting can take many forms, using properties such as shape, size, colour or even male, female or baby animals. A set is any collection of things that have some common property. From sets with a simple property such as colour, one can progress to making sets of other properties such as that of number – for example, piles of three bricks, three dolls or three toy cars. From this the child can be helped to deduce that the threeness is the property that all the sets have in common, and this helps to promote understanding of what is meant by three, in contrast to just learning by heart that it is the number recited after two and before four. From sets with one property the child can move on to sorting out subsets, such as items that are red and long, red and short, blue and long, blue and short, etc.

Many parents have been rather bewildered by the amount of work done with sets in the first years of school, so the importance of sets is best explained in terms of understanding numbers and properties. The basic number rules can all be understood in terms of sets. Combining objects from one set with those from another is the basis of simple addition. The mental process arises out of actually doing the sum physically. A child can combine two bricks in one pile with three bricks in another pile to find out how many there are altogether. This can be portrayed in an exercise book as

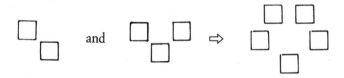

a set of two objects joined to a set of three objects making one set of five objects. Similarly multiplication can be demonstrated as the combination of equivalent sets. Three sets of two makes one set of six, which can be portrayed as

Partitioning or sharing out of sets is a prequel to division. How many subsets of two are in a set of six can be shown pictorially as

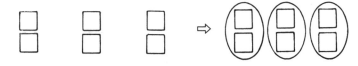

This latter type of manipulation cannot be accomplished until a child can recognise a subset. For example, if one has eight bricks, six of which are red and two blue, ask the child if there are more bricks or more red bricks. A child at an earlier stage of development will invariably reply that there are more red bricks than bricks, and only when he can see that the red bricks are a subset of the total number of bricks can he attempt this form of simple division. Practice can be given in this by getting the child to circle round subsets within a larger group.

In the early years it is important to provide lots of these practical activities with objects like bricks, although as the child makes progress in reading and writing this practical side will gradually diminish. In a large book with pages of plain paper, the parent can easily make up and draw some of these simple numerical problems in a diagrammatical way, to which the child either writes in the answer, gives it orally or draws in objects in the sets left blank. Most children will regard this kind of work as an extension of their play.

How many stars?   Draw 4 boats

Here are 5 cakes

If you eat one, how many are left?
If Daddy eats another, how many are left now?

Draw 4 legs on each dog. How many legs altogether?

Here are some marbles.

Share them equally between Bob and Ben in these bags.

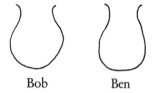

Bob   Ben

Bob has   Ben has

These examples give some idea of the basic number work and sorting that can be devised for young children. A difficult concept that has to be tackled is that of zero. What do we mean by nothing? This can be dealt with by using sets with nothing in them or, for example, by enquiring how many dogs there are in a picture that has no dogs in it.

'Matching' or correspondence is the second mathematical process. It is the principle of matching one to one, which is the foundation of counting. This is typified by putting a cup in each saucer, a shoe on each foot, and is easily practised by laying the cutlery for places at a table. Similar items can be matched out of two piles of objects – for example, matching different colours, sizes or shapes of bricks or Lego, or matching the pictures on picture cards or the dots on dominoes. All this practical work helps establish understanding of the constancy of numbers. This leads to the notion that three books is one more than two books, and thus is important in basic subtraction.

Jane has 3 balls ○○○
John has 4 balls ○○○○
How many balls do you need to take away from John so that he has the same number as Jane?

A lot of this mathematical work can be done orally and understood by children long before they can read or write well enough to deal with such problems in writing. Phrases such as 'more than', 'fewer than' and 'the same number as' can be introduced at this stage.

In a similar way multiplication can be tackled by matching groups – for example, matching groups of two animals going into Noah's ark. Eventually the child can progress in a similar fashion to counting in groups of fives and tens.

I think it can be seen that from the concept of number, sorting into sets and matching by correspondence, all the four basic processes, namely addition, subtraction, multiplication and division, develop. These can all arise out of natural situations, such as how many cakes are left when two have been eaten, or seeing if each doll can be given two cakes when one shares out a whole batch. These combinations can be done physically with actual objects and such manipulation reinforces the basic concepts. Gradually larger numbers can be used, and eventually figures and signs used without pictorial representation. Such words as 'add', 'take away', 'plus', 'equals', 'divide', 'multiply' and 'sum' should be introduced gradually. If all the variations and variables are well practised until the child grasps what he is doing, he will have laid the keystone of all basic number manipulation.

The third mathematical process is that of 'ordering'. This is seen in its simplest form in children's games such as the nest of beakers that fit inside each other or the Russian baboushka dolls. The story of Goldilocks and the Three Bears illustrates the idea of ordering perfectly with little, middle-sized and big bowls, chairs, beds and bears. Almost anything, from pencils to pebbles, can be put in order according to size. Logically from this comes the ordering of numbers into first, second, third, etc.

Ordering leads towards measurement, although with the young child this will not be actual measurement but only developing such ideas as:

longer than	shorter than
wider than	narrower than
fatter than	thinner than
deeper than	shallower than
higher than	lower than

It also helps to distinguish between taller and higher, thin and narrow. All such words should be used correctly and every opportunity taken to compare sizes, contrasting thickness or thinness of lines in drawings or big and small pieces of a puzzle.

Length is the first of these attributes of size that a child understands, and it can be measured with reference to the span of hands or paces of feet. Weight is more difficult than length and not so obvious, as larger objects do not necessarily weigh more than smaller ones and spread-out objects feel lighter than compact objects of the same weight. The grasp of volume and capacity comes at an even later age. Playing at pouring water between different sized containers and with sand buckets on a beach all helps consolidate the notions of size, weight and capacity.

Other notions that can come out of play are those concerned with shape and symmetry. From the baby's simple posting box to sticky paper shapes, there are lots of possibilities for learning the basic shapes of square, rectangle, circle and triangle. Little books can be made for each of the common shapes with pictures cut out of magazines or with drawings, the book of round things including items such as clock faces, wheels, drums, buttons and winches, and that of triangular things – sails and road signs. Practical experience of whether and how things roll can lead to talk of curved as opposed to flat sides. Similarly folding and cutting paper, or folding paper over a blob of wet paint to produce patterns, can lead to simple ideas of symmetry.

Second steps (six to eight years)

If a child has made his own discovery of a mathematical rule by practical means, it will be more firmly embedded in his mind. That is why the emphasis in the early years is on practical activities which often seem like play. During the following years, although practical experience is still valuable, particularly in such fields as weighing and measuring, this will gradually diminish to be replaced by the reading and writing of figures.

Basically the four rules of addition, subtraction, multiplication and division will be consolidated using larger and larger numbers. Identifying numbers up to 10, then 20, 100, 200 will continue on up to 1000.

In addition, the child should learn the constancy of number bonds: that 3 + 4 is the same as 4 + 3 and equally the same as 6 + 1 or 2 + 2 + 2 + 1 or 7 + 0. At some point as the numbers added together increase, the child must learn to carry over from the units to the tens column. This is often best explained practically by exchanging 10 bricks for a larger one of another colour, which can represent ten.

Subtraction is taught alongside addition, as it is the reverse process. A child should be able to understand all the different expressions of the same constant fact, such as that 3 and 2 added together make 5, that 3 taken away from 5 leaves 2 and how many more 5 is than 3.

With subtraction an obstacle to further progress often occurs when the digit to be taken away in the units column is larger than the digit it is being taken from. There are two ways of doing this: by decomposition and by equal addition. In decomposition, a ten is 'borrowed' from the tens column and added to the units:

$$\begin{array}{r} {\scriptstyle(1)} \\ {\scriptstyle(2)}\,\cancel{3}\,2\;- \\ 6 \\ \hline 2\,6 \end{array}$$

In equal addition a ten is added to both sides of the two numbers:

$$\begin{array}{r} \overset{①}{3\ 2} \\ \underline{①\ \ 6} \\ 2\ 6 \end{array}$$

The method used is very much personal preference.

Development of multiplication and division advances rather more slowly, but again these are reverse processes and can be dealt with together. Multiplication is best begun as repeated addition, such as how many are 3 groups of 3, while division is emphasised as a sharing out process, how 16 sweets can be shared between 4 children. Once this is understood, the idea that a remainder might be left over can be introduced. The question of learning multiplication tables has been a disputed topic in recent years and certainly there is little point in learning them before the multiplication process is fully understood – that is, that 4×3 is the same as 3×4, that anything multiplied by 0 will result in 0 and that anything multiplied by 1 will result in no change.

Some of the multiplication tables come as a natural progression from counting in twos, fives or tens, but one of the best ways of comprehending the tables is for the child to discover the number patterns with a number square. The numbers from 1 to 100 are written out in a square of tens and then every second, fifth, seventh or whatever number is chosen is outlined or coloured in a different colour. Looking at the pattern formed for each number is not only a great aid to understanding multiplication but a useful prelude to learning each table.

```
 1   2   3  ④   5   6   7  ⑧   9  10
11  ⑫  13  14  15  ⑯  17  18  19  ⑳
21  22  23  ㉔  25  26  27  ㉘  29  30
31  ㉜  33  34  35  ㊱  37  38  39  ㊵
41  42  43  ㊹  45  46  47  ㊽  49  50
51  ㊼  53  54  55  ㊻  57  58  59  ⑥⓪
61  62  63  ㊽  65  66  67  ㊻  69  70
71  ㊽  73  74  75  ㊼  77  78  79  ⑧⓪
81  82  83  ⑧④  85  86  87  ⑧⑧  89  90
91  ㊽  93  94  95  ㊻  97  98  99  ⑩⓪
```

Number square showing the pattern of the 4 × table.

At this age group, the four number processes can also be applied to money, to very simple fractions such as a half and a quarter, and to measurements. Although measurement might begin by relating sizes to the body with spans or paces, children quickly see the advantage of using the more standard ruler or tape measure. A balance for the simple weighing of objects is a great aid, although many galleys may not have such equipment and so will have to be content with estimations of heavy and light. Shopping expeditions can also help with the idea of standard measures of weight. Many galleys, however, might have a measuring jug, which can be used for work on capacity.

Money might conceivably present a problem when changing from one currency to another, although I have found that children usually master very quickly what is to their advantage, such as how much pocket money they are due to receive, and in practice currency changes rarely present any problems.

Around this age a child will be learning to tell the time. A toy clock on which the hands can be moved is useful, or alternatively one can draw clock faces in the child's number book and get him to mark in the hands for various times. First the child learns the hours, then half hours, quarter hours and minutes, progressing to the idea of *to* the hour and *past* the hour. It is difficult to teach the minutes until a child is able to count proficiently in fives.

Junior level (eight to twelve years)

In mathematics there is a definite progression and some children will move smoothly ahead all the time. This is probably more the case when being taught on a one-to-one basis, where boring repetitive work can be cut out and any difficulties are speedily dealt with. At this junior level age, individually taught children often surge forward rapidly. It is important, however, to check continually that they do understand what they are doing and so are building on firm foundations. It pays to keep an eye open for any block or particular difficulty. Some children make spurts when they grasp an idea and seem to progress in fits and starts, occasionally appearing to stand still for a while. Parents should be reassured that this is quite normal. Nevertheless it is important to keep a careful record of what work a child has completed successfully.

The main work at this age is building on what has gone before; there are not many new concepts, but there is a great extension of the old ones. In number work, the child will move on to manipulating larger and larger numbers. He should understand even and odd numbering, the ordinal and cardinal numbers, and what place value – the fact that the figure 2 stands for different amounts when it is in different places in a number – means. Children often enjoy learning the Roman numerals and ways of numbering in other cultures, and this is a good age at which to introduce some historical ideas of number.

In the four basic processes, the child will move on to using numbers of more digits. In addition, not only numbers of more digits but more sets of such numbers will be added. In subtraction, multidigit numbers will be used in stages, first without and then with equal addition or decomposition. If one can see that the child easily masters this progression there is no need to do rows and rows of examples with bigger and yet bigger numbers.

In multiplication, a child will progress to number patterns and a tables square, which he can construct himself as he learns each individual table.

```
 1  2  3  4  5  6  7  8  9 10
 2  4  6  8 10 12 14 16 18 20
 3  6  9 12 15 18 21 24 27 30
 4  8 12 16 20 24 28 32 36 40
 5 10 15 20 25 30 35 40 45 50
 6 12 18 24 30 36 42 48 54 60
 7 14 21 28 35 42 49 56 63 70
 8 16 24 32 40 48 56 64 72 80
 9 18 27 36 45 54 63 72 81 90
10 20 30 40 50 60 70 80 90 100
```

Tables Square.

One major step in multiplication is the point at which a figure must be carried over into the tens or hundreds column, for example:

$$\begin{array}{c} 15 \\ \underline{6\times} \\ 90 \end{array} \qquad \text{as opposed to the simple} \qquad \begin{array}{c} 11 \\ \underline{3\times} \\ 33 \end{array}$$

There are basically two ways of tackling division, by sharing 30 cakes among 6 girls, or by seeing how many girls will each have 5 cakes out of a total of 30. Division can be set out in two ways, the choice of which is a matter of personal preference.

$$\begin{array}{c} 5 \\ 6\overline{)30} \end{array} \qquad \begin{array}{c} 6\overline{)30} \\ 5 \end{array}$$

Firstly units are divided by units, then tens and units by units, and finally hundreds, tens and units by units.

Many people feel that teaching long multiplication and long division is redundant in the age of the pocket calculator, but others still prefer to teach it to children who are interested. There are almost two schools of thought as regards computation: those who think constant practice makes perfect and those who think too much practice has a negative effect. A way of defeating this is to introduce more interesting numerical problems for the child to find the answers to instead of repetitive examples.

Starting with halves and quarters, fractions can be given practical emphasis by cutting and folding paper, and using money parallels, such as a half or quarter of a dollar. The order of introducing fractions is $\frac{1}{2}$, $\frac{1}{4}$, $\frac{3}{4}$ and $\frac{1}{10}$. Important concepts for the child to realise in fractions are those of size, namely that $\frac{1}{10}$ is smaller than $\frac{1}{4}$, and also equivalence, that $\frac{4}{8}$ is the same as $\frac{1}{2}$. This latter is easily demonstrated by cutting a paper circle into eight portions.

Learning the name for numerator and denominator, a child can be shown how to change a top-heavy fraction or improper fraction, for example $\frac{11}{4}$ into a mixed number $2\frac{3}{4}$. Simple fractions can be added and subtracted at this stage using the lowest common denominator (that is, the lowest number into which both numbers will go). For example:

$$\frac{1}{2} + \frac{1}{3} = \frac{3+2}{6} = \frac{5}{6}$$

At the same time a child should be introduced to the idea of decimals and learn their fractional equivalents (that is, $\frac{1}{10} = 0.1$ and $\frac{1}{2} = 0.5$) and how to convert one to the other.

In measurement, the various standard units of length, weight and capacity will be used and manipulated, using the four number processes, fractions and decimal notation. Carrying on from this one can progress to making simple plans, first without and then with a scale. Area is best explained by 'tiling' – the number of small squares which will fit over the space to be measured. Whether one measures in pints or litres, the idea of capacity is one of the hardest for a child to grasp. Using a measuring jug is useful for discovering in a practical way that a pint is a pint; whatever shape of container it is poured into, tall and thin or short and fat, does not matter – the amount of liquid stays the same.

The child should now be able to tell the time to the minute and work out practical problems involving time, such as how many hours of schoolwork he does if he starts at 10.30 am and finishes at 1 pm. At this age he should understand and be able to use a calendar, timetable and diary. Children often become fascinated by other methods of measuring time, such as sundials or eggtimers, and also enjoy using stopwatches. On a boat it is quite easy to explain the 24 hour clock and geographical aspects of time, especially if the child has the experience of travelling from one time zone to another. The practical implications of time are all too evident to the sailor.

Working with shapes, the child can learn simple aspects of geometry and should become familiar with such shapes as hexagons, pentagons, cubes and cones as well as the simpler shapes. Discussion of the properties of shapes should include right angles, parallel lines, equal sides and angles. Discovering some of the rules of geometry, by practical work with shapes, now usually takes place much earlier than it once did. In the past geometry was introduced at a later age, in an abstract way with hypotheses and theorems. For example, by taking various paper shapes of isosceles triangles with both acute and obtuse apex angles, a child can discover by folding these shapes that the base angles fit each other and so are equal, that an axis of symmetry cuts the base line into two equal parts, and that this axis also cuts the angle at the apex into two equal parts. Folding and cutting shapes can demonstrate much about geometry and symmetry without having to do formal proofs.

Averages, percentages, ratios and proportion are other topics that a child can work on during this period; also how to construct simple graphs and charts from measurements, say by using a thermometer, barometer or wind speed indicator, as shown in the chapter about amusing a child on passage (Chapter 8).

Senior level (over twelve years)

In this chapter I have tried to outline very briefly the main aspects of mathematics to be covered, putting most of the emphasis on the earlier years. I recommended that for older children it is probably essential to work from a book of some kind as it is far too time-consuming for the parent to both make up and provide the answers for mathematical problems. In the scope of this chapter all I shall do is outline the most important topics that a child should cover before the end of his secondary education, which may be useful for a parent checking through a book or a correspondence course.

The course should include the four number processes and work in different bases, fractions and decimals, squares, indices and square roots. Measurement should include conversion between units, perimeter, area and volume of shapes. Ratio, proportion, scale, percentages and averages should also be covered. In algebra, equations will usually be solved in various ways, such as simultaneous, quadratic and linear. Symmetry, angles and parallels, similarity and congruence of geometrical shapes, the features of circles, arcs and sectors will also be studied. Nowadays logarithms are scarcely touched upon, although trigonometry appears to be holding its own and is useful to a budding navigator. The graphical representation of data is also important, as are the features of a straight line graph and the use of coordinates. These are probably the most important topics, although there are plenty of others, such as matrices, vectors and probability, which are included in senior courses.

In conclusion, I would like to stress once more how vital mathematics is and that it is a subject which must be paid its full due in the schoolroom afloat. It is not, however, quite as formidable as it may seem, and in this chapter I have tried to simplify some of the thinking that goes into the teaching of mathematics and have stressed the importance of the early years. Guiding a child along the path to understanding mathematics is no more difficult than learning the concepts that underlie navigation, and every boat has, or should have, a navigator on board. He or she might be the ideal person to take charge of the mathematics lessons.

16
Using the Environment

The frontiers of knowledge are expanding so rapidly and encompassing so much that no one can possibly know about everything. Our obligation to our children is to ensure that they are literate and numerate, but apart from these basic skills, the other fields of learning are wide open. This is the real pleasure and joy in cruising: the opportunity it offers for children to learn about the world around them. I have used the word 'learn' deliberately, for this should be a voyage of discovery for the child, not a handing down of secondhand experiences 'taught' by an adult. Learning does not have to take place in a school building and during certain school hours, separate from the rest of life. Children can learn a great deal by having access to the real world, along with time and space to think over what they have observed and experienced in it.

Every area where one can cruise has something to offer, whether it be history, natural beauty, wildlife or folk customs. In most places there will be an overlap of subject matters, for rarely do these fall into neat compartments of history, geography or nature study; nor is there any particular virtue in studying these different disciplines in isolation. To make the most of their experiences, children will need some direction, a framework within which to work and constant encouragement. The parent's guidance and suggestions will be necessary, whether in providing relevant books, or helping the child to search for the information he needs. The plant needs to be watered and fed in order to blossom.

The simplest way to deal with subjects is to make a special folder for a particular country or area cruised in. This folder can include work on many different facets, as well as descriptions of places visited or things seen. It can easily incorporate any special interest a child has. As mentioned earlier in the chapter on a holiday cruise, this topic work can be carried out whether one is cruising for a short period or a lengthy one. (In fact, for a shorter cruise, a project of this nature is almost all that need be done, apart from some mathematics, as such a project would incorporate both writing and reading skills.) Not everything has to be recorded in writing, for it is sometimes equally valuable to look at and discuss things without the strain of having to write everything down, especially for younger children. The experience is more important than the recording of it.

As part of our school programme, my children kept folders on every major area we cruised in, and by examining some of these areas in more detail and the kind of school work we did there, I hope to illustrate the way that the cruising environment can be used for an educational purpose. This work is not just educational, because these folders can give lasting pleasure, being looked at, reread and enjoyed when the child is older, to bring to life his memories of a cruise.

Greece

We first started our cruising life in the Mediterranean, which is a treasure trove of history and legend, so that it was never difficult to find topics of interest. Two summers were spent in Greece, which has always been a popular cruising ground and still is today, especially since the increase in flotilla sailing holidays.

The first thing I ensured was that we had plenty of reading material: an illustrated children's book on aspects of modern Greece, but more important, a large selection of the tales and legends of ancient Greece. There are several versions which retell the stories of the Greek heroes and gods for children, and fortunately some of these are in lightweight paperback editions. Roger Lancelyn Green is one author highly recommended, who has retold the story of Troy as well as other legends. While Green's books require a certain reading proficiency, some simpler books for younger children also retell famous legends such as that of Theseus and the Minotaur. All these stories, from the wooden horse of Troy to Jason and the Golden Fleece or the labours of Hercules, are great stories enjoyed by children of all ages. Older children might like to dip into adult books and a good guide to the area, such as *Hellenic Traveller* by Guy Pentreath or *Collins Companion Guide to the Greek Islands* can also be an asset to the cruising bookshelf. Snippets of interesting information about places visited are also to be found in the sea-guides written by H.M. Denham. There is a reasonable selection of children's books in English on sale at several bookshops in Athens and other major tourist centres.

Reading the stories of the gods and heroes made our voyaging all that much more enjoyable, and not only for the children. Often we just read the stories and talked about them, especially when visiting the places described, as when in the wake of Odysseus we sailed past several whirlpools in the Messina Straits, trying to guess which ones were Scylla and Charybdis. Identifying places mentioned in the *Odyssey* became a guessing game we all played as we sailed around the Mediterranean. Odysseus' ten years of wanderings among the islands on his voyage home from Troy captured Doina's imagination particularly. When we visited Troy, she sat immobile on the thick walls of the ruins gazing out across the plain. 'Just imagine, this is where Helen herself might have stood and watched the battles,' she whispered in awe. Fields of waving corn stretched down to the Aegean Sea, where once a thousand Greek ships had been at anchor. On that plain a hundred thousand soldiers had camped, and it was where Achilles and Hector had locked in deadly battle. From the vantage point of Troy on its hill, it was easy to see why it had been difficult for the attackers to catch the city unawares and why they had to resort to a trick such as the wooden horse.

At other ruins, high on the hill overlooking Pylos Bay and the island of

In Greece, schoolwork often consisted of looking at what was around us. Here *Aventura* motors between the steep cut sides of the old Corinth Canal.

Sphacteria, I read out to the children part of Thucydides' contemporary account of the battles that had raged there during the Peloponnesian War two thousand years previously. A general in that war, Thucydides had written a factual account of the battles between the armies of Athens and Sparta for this steepsided stronghold, now thick with trees. It was exciting to read about the events when sitting looking at the place where it had all happened. The passage describing the narrow entrance to the harbour behind the island where ships had been strung across to block it was so vivid that it took little stretch of the imagination to hear swords clashing and ships ramming each other. After reading about this battle, the next day in our schoolwork we found out exactly what a 'hoplite' soldier was, how he dressed and what weapons he used. A drawing of a hoplite with round shield, leg guards, bronze helmet and spear was duly added to the Greek folder.

Not so very far away we crossed the track of Homer's *Odyssey* once again as we visited the ruins of Nestor's palace at ancient Pylos. For centuries the *Odyssey* was regarded as an invention of the author, but gradually more and more evidence has arisen to show that it was in fact based on truth. Professor Blegen of Cincinnati had decided that, if Homer was right, Nestor's palace must be somewhere in this area, and after much searching he eventually unearthed it. There is not a great deal of the walls left, but Doina was extremely excited by the decorated bath near the entrance and beside the throne room, for in the *Odyssey* it is described how when Odysseus' son comes to Nestor's palace looking for his father, he is given a bath and anointed with oil by the king's daughter. This then involved us in a discussion about ceremonies and rituals for receiving visitors in ancient times, for the idea of a princess personally giving a visitor a bath had caught the children's imagination.

Almost every Greek island has something of interest to offer, from Apollo's birthplace on the sacred isle of Delos, to the cave where St John had his Revelation on Patmos, or catacombs of over a thousand early Christian burial vaults running in spooky tunnels into the hillside on the island of Milos. Often schoolwork simply took the form of writing about the place visited, which helped to fix the facts observed more indelibly. Our folders on Greece did not include only accounts of history and legend, but also aspects of modern Greece and the way of life of its present day inhabitants, such as typical food dishes, fruits and cakes, the Greek flag and what it stood for, the Greek alphabet and its English equivalents, plus a list of some of the Greek words that the children had learnt. In some places we bought postcards to stick in the folder or cut the photographs out of tourist brochures, with the children also drawing both what they had seen, such as big jars used for storing oil, and from their imagination, such as Medusa with her snake hair. Wherever we cruised in Greece, the historical past beckoned, so that it was almost impossible to ignore it.

The amount of depth that can be given to historical studies depends very much on the age of the child. The idea of time develops only very slowly as a child matures and to understand history a child has to have at least some sense of the past. Even so, a child will understand long before he can verbalise what it is he understands, and this understanding is encouraged by giving the child glimpses of the past to draw on. By looking at old objects and places, children can begin to see how history is a deduction about life in the past based on the evidence which has survived; how digging things up from under the earth gives clues as to the way people used to live. The element of detective work and puzzling out of clues that archeology involves has an appeal for most children. Until secondary age is reached almost all that a child will grasp is that these events and style of life happened a long while ago, and only at a later age will they be able to make abstractions beyond this concrete evidence in order to grasp historical perspective.

Even if a young child cannot grasp the time span involved, he can enjoy as much as an older child the wonder of some of the treasures of the past. Encouraging this sense of wonder and enjoyment is probably the most important thing a parent can do, creating an interest that will flourish later on in life. Of course, as in any field, one can push too hard and a surfeit of old ruins and yet another Greek amphitheatre can get to be a little too much for a young child. My own children usually let me know when I had reached their limit, with sly comments about mother doing another of her 'readings from the classics' routine.

For both young and old, a high point in our cruising in Greek waters was our visit to the palace of King Minos at Knossos in Crete, while we were anchored in the old Venetian port of Iraklion, even if our young children did not grasp that Knossos was at least a thousand years older than most of the other ruins we had seen. The story of Theseus and the Minotaur had been read by both children over and over again.

Minos was a powerful king who kept a monster bull, called the Minotaur, in the intricate labyrinth under his palace. Every year mainland Greek towns such as Athens had to send some of their finest young men and women to be sacrificed to appease this bull. One year the Prince Theseus was among those sent, but Minos' daughter Ariadne fell in love with him and decided to save him. In short, Theseus killed the Minotaur and found his way out of the labyrinth by using the ball of string that Ariadne had thoughtfully given him.

The palace at Knossos is enormous, full of royal apartments, reception rooms and storerooms containing row upon row of huge earthenware jars for oil or wine, some taller than a fully grown man. There were bathrooms and a laundry, a throne room with the oldest throne in Europe, corridors and staircases, for the main palace was several storeys high. The brightly coloured wall paintings had been removed to the museum, but had been replaced with good copies. Ivan was fascinated by a painting that showed young men and women somersaulting over a bull. They appeared to rush up to the bull, grab it by the horns, do an acrobatic somersault over its back and land on the ground beside it. Apparently bull leaping was a great test of nerve and daring. Doina's favourite room was the queen's bathroom, which had walls painted a vivid blue, along which swam dolphins, many different kinds of fish and other sea creatures. She became so rapt in the fresco that she failed to notice which way the rest of us had gone, and left by the opposite door. Lost, she turned back to look for us, while we took other turnings in our search for her. Up and down stairs, passages twisted in every direction, narrow and winding several times before they came to dead ends and one had to turn back. It was a real labyrinth. When we eventually found Doina, she was quite frightened and admitted that she had started to hear the Minotaur roaring. The legend had become a reality never to be forgotten.

In the museum, among all the treasures found in the palace, there were bulls everywhere: a big bull's head of solid gold, paintings of bulls, bulls leaping around vases, even tiny gold earrings with bulls' heads engraved on them, three thousand years old. The children were very curious as to why the Minoans had been so obsessed by bulls. They listened quite rapt to the prevailing theory that the rumbling sounds heard during the earthquakes that the region was prone to were explained as being due to a monster bull under the earth. The sacrifices of the youths and maidens were intended to keep the bull quiet, but it was to little avail as most experts agree that the Minoan civilisation was indeed destroyed by a large earthquake. The story so fascinated the two young children that they had to be almost dragged from the museum at closing time.

The Ancient Greeks used stories to explain the mysteries of nature. If there was thunder, it was a god being angry and throwing a thunderbolt. Storms at sea were Poseidon, the god of the seas being angry. The Greek gods looked and behaved like human beings. In the old days poets would tell the stories of the heroes. Some of the heroes were real people but it all happened so long ago, that the poets made up exciting stories about what the heroes did.

This was eight year old Doina's explanation in her Greek folder.

When not crossing the path of the hero Odysseus, we seemed to be following in the wake of St Paul, who crisscrossed the Mediterranean in his many missionary journeys. The description in the Acts of the Apostles of Paul facing the irate mob in the huge amphitheatre at Ephesus was another passage we read on site to conjure up the past. From Ephesus, easily reached from the marina at Kusadasi, the entire Turkish coast southwards is a wonderland for the sea-based explorer, as remains of so many civilisations and epochs lay scattered along its shore. The isolation of this area from the rest of Turkey is explained by the mountains rising thousands of feet behind the narrow coastal strip. Large Roman tombs stand rakishly askance on the shores of remote bays, a single Byzantine arch of an early church adorns a small beach, while the swimmer can

185

discover the remains of houses fronting old harbours that now lie in clear waters near to the anchor. In Andraki, we went by dinghy a mile or two up the river before reaching the old port of Myra, which like Ephesus had once been on the sea but was no more. History was turning into geography as the effects of the sea encroaching or rivers silting were plain to see, or could be easily seen on the plains!

The Caribbean

In some cruising areas the natural environment dominated our schoolwork, often as a counterbalance to an overdose of the historical. The Caribbean was our first acquaintance with the tropics, a new world of different vegetation, fruits and vegetables, as well as the splendours to be found underwater, after the often sterile Mediterranean waters.

A typical project was the exploration of a small deserted island near to our anchorage in the islands north of Grenada. In the nature of an expedition, we collected specimens, such as leaves from the trees, or samples of the sand, made a note of everything we discovered and finally with snorkels and masks explored the coral reef. Back in our floating schoolroom, the children recorded their work, firstly by drawing a sketch plan of the island and colouring the beach area yellow, the sea blue, the reef brown and the small hill on the island green. Also on this map they marked an enormous pile of shells and a circle of stones placed around the traces of a fire, both evidence of fishermen's activity that had intrigued the children. The mound of conch shells was several metres high and according to Doina's calculations contained over a million of the large shells, every one unfortunately spoiled with a slit cut into it where the fishermen had removed the lambi, a much prized local delicacy. We also discovered two artificially created pools, probably for keeping fish or lobsters in. Some of the plants we collected were pressed and stuck onto sheets of paper, while rubbings were taken of the bigger leaves with coloured crayons. Various shells gathered were also drawn and coloured, as was an old bird's nest found in a tree.

When Doina inspected the sand closely, she found it was made up of minute pieces of broken coral. Carefully, she separated out her sample into the differently coloured grains, white, pink, black, brown and green, sticking each type carefully on her page under transparent adhesive tape. The reef had been a little disappointing, having few fish and a lot of dead coral, but in other places we collected some of the different sorts of coral, millepore, star, brain or branched. This prompted the children to read about what kind of animal coral is and how it builds up the large reefs, one of Nature's amazing stories.

Older children can extend this kind of work into trying to identify shells, fish or plants found – if not the species, at least the families to which they belong.

This can be developed into writing about some of the more interesting characteristics of an animal or family. Small reference books on marine life, shells or birds are therefore invaluable to have on board. As flora and fauna vary so much from region to region, it is often a good idea to buy these books locally.

A great advantage of the English language is that books are readily available in most parts of the world. One relic left by the far flung British Empire is that in many ex-colonies the education system has remained in English, even if only from the secondary level upwards. So in many places it is possible to buy school textbooks especially published for that particular region, for example, *A Visual History of the West Indies* by Sheila Duncker, which I purchased in Grenada, or *Stories of Pacific People* edited by B. Cahill, which I bought in Fiji. The latter was very useful as it had questions to answer at the end of each chapter and also suggestions for things to do. The local bookshops are well worth delving into, and in many countries there are also good secondhand bookshops to browse through. In Israel, for example, we found an exchange bookshop where we could offload some of our books in exchange for other books at little cost.

United States of America

In the United States, of course, we had little difficulty in laying our hands on reading material, or finding work to do using the environment we were sailing through. Starting our cruise in Florida's waterways, the wildness of marsh and lagoon, thick with a multitude of different water birds, with glimpses of the unique manatee surfacing for air, contrasted to our visits to the Space Center at Cape Canaveral or Disney World. Having sailed from England ourselves in a small boat, it was easy to step into the shoes of the Pilgrim Fathers when we visited the replica of the *Mayflower* at Plymouth. The coast of New England is rich in historical associations, where many old buildings grace towns such as Marblehead or Portsmouth. On Newcastle Island in New Hampshire, the old William and Mary fort looks out over the harbour, marking the first victory over the British at the beginning of the Revolution. In visiting Boston and by reading the story of the Boston tea party, early American history and the War of Independence figured large in our schoolwork, which culminated in witnessing the Fourth of July celebrations in New York. Very instructive were the many houses and other buildings open to the public, such as the house of the polar explorer Robert Peary, on Eagle Island in Maine, or the small museums in seaside towns, such as that of Provincetown, which had many fascinating exhibits about whaling, boats and the fishing industry.

The museums everywhere in the United States I found to be of great value, for on the whole the exhibits were well displayed, labelled and with good explanatory descriptions. Many museums also had exhibits targeted at the

At Mystic Seaport, the whaling ship *Charles W. Morgan* makes schoolwork more interesting.

younger generation, which could be touched or manipulated, or else ran film shows or demonstrations. The pride of place goes to Mystic Seaport, a reconstruction of a nineteenth century seaport, where we spent several days and which is one of the most fascinating museums in the world. Reached by sailing up the winding Mystic river, one can actually dock in the museum close to old sailing boats, a whaling ship, the *Joseph Conrad* and other historic vessels. Houses and shops line the quay and streets, for this is not only a museum but a working one, and all maintenance and restoration of old boats is carried out in the museum workshops in the traditional manner, museum attendants being clad in nineteenth century costume. The rope walk, rigging shop, smithy and sail loft are all in working order and the craftsmen only too willing to chat about their skills. Knowledgeable staff cook old recipes over open fireplaces, roll pills by hand in the pharmacy, carve figureheads and etch scrimshaw. There are also standard museum exhibits on display, as well as talks on such topics as whaling, illustrated with old films. In a special children's section built in a replica of a captain's cabin, the children could try on clothes and play with toys that children would have used a hundred years ago, as well as read accounts of life on board, for many of the old time sailing captains took their families to sea with them.

On the evening we arrived, I walked around the museum and noted things of interest. From this I compiled a list of things for the children to find out, draw and do; then I wrote these out onto sheets of paper, leaving space for their answers or drawings. During the following two days the children were dispatched with these sheets on clipboards as their school work. Typical questions given to eight year old Ivan were:

- Describe the *Emma C. Berry* and her rig.
- Where did *Glory Anna II* come from?
- What is her rig?
- Choose one boat from the Small Boat Shop. Describe and draw it.
- *Charles W. Morgan*, whaling ship. Find out:
  When and where she was built
  How long she is
  How many masts and how many yardarms she has.
  What code flags she flies and why.
- Describe what you can see in the William White Rigging Loft.
- James Driggs Shipsmith Shop. What did a shipsmith do?
- What is a mast hoop?
- Choose another building and describe exactly what you see in it.
- In the children's museum, describe the life of the children who went to sea, where they slept, what they did, their toys, etc. How does it differ from your life?

This clipboard quiz was a technique I used frequently, not only in museums or aquariums, but also in some of the harbours, as a means of keeping the children's interest aroused. They always enjoyed the opportunity to get off the boat and work ashore with clipboards, rather than down below on our main cabin table.

In the wake of those who sailed before

Before the advent of the aeroplane, the seas were the great thoroughfares of the world, so wherever one sails, one is almost always sailing in the wake of someone whose story has been recorded either by himself or by others. Many of these stories are not too difficult for children to read in the original, but also there are accounts of the voyages of such sailors as Columbus written especially for children. These make very good reading on a passage, as do books about the destination. In this way we all read Thor Heyerdahl's *The Kon Tiki Expedition* and *Aku Aku* on our three week passage to Easter Island and debated the possibilities of raft voyages from South America and the origins of the Easter Island statues.

On the way to Pitcairn Island we soaked up the story of the mutiny on the *Bounty*, Captain Bligh's small-boat voyage across the Pacific and an account of the violence and intrigue of the mutineers' early years on Pitcairn. The pleasant Pitcairners were almost a disappointment when they turned out not to be swashbuckling buccaneers. Captain Cook made his presence felt from Tahiti to Australia, while in Samoa we trekked up Mount Vaea to the tomb of Robert Louis Stevenson, 'under the wide and starry sky'. Historical figures such as these are one way to interest a child in the past and places visited while, for example, studying the voyage of Captain Cook, and the observations he made can lead onto work on geographical skills, navigation and map and chart making.

Many of the geographical concepts to do with climate, weather and location can easily be studied on a boat, wherever one happens to be sailing. This can start from weather observations and progress to considering the sun, earth, moon and planets and their movements, the seasons, the composition of the atmosphere, how winds arise, cloud formations, aspects of the earth's curvature such as the horizon, meridians, the poles, latitude and longitude. The starting point can be any phenomenon observed, as happened to us one day when we saw a rare halo around the sun. An interesting exercise is to try and make a chart of an anchorage, using a leadline for sounding the depths, a simple leadline being easily made with any weights and line. A child soon comes to appreciate that chart making is not an easy task. Many of the geographical topics are understood quite

Ivan measures up to one of the mysterious statues on Easter Island.

readily by a child who is living so close to Nature in a marine environment. Many points, such as the curvature of the earth, can be demonstrated by the way things appear over the horizon – the funnel before the ship or the palm trees before the atoll. This work is helped by the fact that most sailing children are interested in finding out more about these subjects which impinge so obviously upon their lives.

In this chapter I have drawn extensively on my own experiences to illustrate some of the subjects which can be used to help a child learn about the world we live in. There are many more that I have not the space to touch on, for every place has something to offer if one bothers to look for it. Even where there is little history written down, such as in many remoter areas of the Pacific, where what happened in the 'time before' was passed on orally to people living in 'time now', there is much a child can discover by observing and recording traditions and customs of other people's ways of life. There are a myriad of things to do, observe and read about, waiting to be discovered, wherever one points one's bow, for this is the zenith of education afloat.

Books

(1963) *Collins Companion Guide to the Greek Islands*. London: Collins.
Cahill, B. *ed*. (1972) *Stories of Pacific People*. Hong Kong: Longman Group.
Denham, H. M. (1970) *The Aegean*. London: John Murray.
Denham, H. M. (1972) *The Ionian Islands to Rhodes*. London: John Murray.
    (See also other sea guides by H. M. Denham.)
Duncker, S. (1975) *A Visual History of the West Indies*. London: Evans Bros.
Green, R. L. (1958) *Tales of Greek Heroes*. London: Puffin Books.
Green, R. L. (1958) *The Tale of Troy*. London: Puffin Books.
Heyerdahl, T. (1960) *The Kon Tiki Expedition*. London: Penguin Books.
Heyerdahl, T. (1963) *Aku Aku*. London: Penguin Books.
Lines, K. *ed*. (1973) *The Faber Book of Greek Legends*. London: Faber & Faber.
Pentreath, G. (1971) *Hellenic Traveller*. London: Faber & Faber.
Ridgell, R. (1982) *Pacific Nations and Territories*. Guam: Guam Community College, PO Box 23069, Guam 96921.
Warner, R. (*trans*.) (1972) *Thucydides' The Peloponnesian War*. London: Penguin Books.

17
An Approach to Science

At first sight, teaching scientific subjects on a boat appears a little difficult, especially with older children. The obvious obstacle is the lack of any laboratory facilities or specialised equipment such as microscopes, which schools ashore usually possess. This applies equally to those following correspondence courses, who may have difficulty carrying out some of the practical work specified in their course. However there are plenty of opportunities for scientific study in the sailing environment, provided one uses a little ingenuity.

It is not possible to cover the whole range of scientific knowledge, nor is it necessary to deal with every topic. The important thing is to nurture certain principles and a scientific way of doing things and finding things out. The aim of science is to understand the world we live in by means of observation and investigation. This scientific observation of how objects behave under various conditions and the similarities and differences between them is the basis from which to work. One is interested in observation, not impressions; fact not fiction. A child should be encouraged to record accurately how things are and how they change, to observe, question and experiment, so as to be able to draw some conclusions. The basic scientific approach is to ask questions to form a theory, then test by experimentation to see if this theory is justified.

Although it is fairly obvious that children learn by discovery, it is not sufficient to hope that they will understand principles just by their own observations and experiments, whether it is to see if objects float or sink, dissolve, make sounds or can fly. Although all such properties can be tested and explored, it does not mean that the theory behind the observation will be learned. This may well need some help from an adult or book, usually in the form of asking leading questions or prodding the child towards the right conclusion.

Scientific knowledge does not fall neatly into separate compartments, and there is little point on a boat in making divisions between the sciences of physics, chemistry, biology, meteorology, astronomy and so on until a child is well on the way to specialisation at a later age. For example, work on sound waves (physics) can be done at the same time as a study of the ear and how we hear (biology). Obviously there will be an overlap with aspects of the environmental, geographical and nature studies discussed in the previous chapter. Science has slow beginnings and for the younger child much of the work done in mathematics, such as measuring and weighing, can also be regarded as falling into the scientific arena. There is much to be said for letting a child follow particular topics that interest him in the scientific field, but it is also important to bring to his notice other ideas which he may have no way of discovering on his own.

I have found many of the science books written for the junior school level rather disappointing – either far too simplistic, or else far too ambitious, difficult to follow even ashore when plenty of equipment is available. Before buying any textbooks, do look through them very carefully and see if it will be possible to follow the programme laid out, taking into account what equipment is available. It is possible to do a lot of experiments using ordinary items found on most boats or with simple items easily bought. In the following pages I shall outline some suggestions for practical work.

Infants

The very young child will still be developing some basic concepts which are dealt with in mathematics, so very little work of a pure scientific nature can be done. A beginning towards science can be made by looking at the similarities and differences between various objects in respect of their size, colour or texture. The senses of sight, hearing, touch, taste and smell can all be explored to reinforce the child's observations. By making collections of similar things – flowers, shells, stamps or whatever – the child can start to develop an idea of classification. This can be promoted further by considering the differences between living and non-living things. The child should be able to point out some of the different characteristics of birds, animals, fish or insects. Lists of these properties can be made as a child decides what family to put a particular creature into. Similarly one can provide various objects which the child has to put into some classification, such as those that float and those that sink, recording the results on a sheet of paper divided into two halves, for floaters and sinkers. Encouraging

193

the child to guess first and then, after seeing the result, asking him why he made a particular guess, helps the child to formulate ideas of weight and displacement. This is especially important when the child guessed wrongly.

Middle years

The important principles to develop at this age are careful, accurate description and observation, the attitude of questioning, and not accepting an answer without proof.

Most children take a lively interest in living things and should be able to distinguish the characteristics of the main animal groupings of insects, fish, birds, reptiles and mammals; they should know about their life cycles, ways of life, and how they move. Within an animal family, some of the ways the members differ according to their different modes of life can be considered. For example, among the birds, the different kinds of feet, talons and claws can be written about and drawn: the long thin claws of birds that cling to rocks, the larger splayed claws of perching birds, the doglike feet of running birds, the sharp curved talons of birds of prey, the webbed feet of water birds or the backward-facing toes on the feet of tree-climbing birds. Watching birds gathering to

Careful observation is the basis of scientific study. Giant turtles on the beach in Bali provide a practical opportunity for Ivan.

194

migrate or even receiving visits from migrating birds coming to rest on one's boat, as we did on several occasions, can lead to work on migration, its patterns and reasons.

The life cycles of insects such as butterflies, and the way ants and bees live and work, fascinate most children, although it might be impossible to observe these phenomena directly. Any insect or butterfly, caught maybe with a fishing net, can be carefully drawn and described. A small magnifying glass or hand lens can be very useful here.

Similarly the characteristic parts of fish – fins, gills and scales – can be described and drawn, as well as those of other marine animals, such as the octopus or starfish, and descriptions written of what they eat or where they live. Any creature that is found can be written about, emphasising a careful scientific description and encouraging the child to identify the animal or plant in a reference book.

This is Doina's description of the pretty blue animals we fished out of the sea one day:

Velella Velella

Yesterday it was calm, and so we could see the By-the-Wind Sailors floating by. At first we didn't know what they were, so Mummy manoeuvred the boat around, while Ivan and I tried to get one with a butterfly net. In the end we got one and identified it. This was on the way to Pitcairn Island ... in the south east Pacific. By-the-Wind Sailors are kinds of jellyfish, they are relatives of the Portuguese Man o'War. It is a 'cnidarian' because it has stinging cells. Its class is Hydrazoa. Its group is called 'sailing siphonophores'.

Velella Vellellas only sail over tropical and subtropical parts of ocean. The jelly-like base is an ellipse, so if one end is North and the other end is South, the sail points from SE to NW. In other parts of the Pacific, the sail points from SW to NE.

The base is a very dark blue and the crest-like sail is transparent. It is about 5 cm long and 3 cm wide. At the bottom is a fairly big hole covered in tentacles. There is a small space, which is probably the mouth. The By-the-Wind Sailors eat as they sail along. Plankton are stunned by the stinging cells and are passed into its mouth by the mobile tentacles.

Similarly various flowers can be taken to pieces to find out what they have in common and an accurate drawing and description made, labelling parts such as petals, stamen and stigma. As well as individual plants or animals, some general ideas might be examined, such as the tracks and signs that animals leave behind: footprints and tracks on sand or earth, signs of their eating (snail shells cracked open, empty crab claws or nut shells), their droppings, lost feathers or their homes such as nests. Some of these clues could be looked for during a walk ashore. The different kinds of seeds and how they disperse, the ways that animals camouflage or protect themselves (stings, bites, ink-clouds) are other topics that could be explored.

At some point it is logical to move on to looking at the human and what makes us different from the rest of the animals. Nearly all children are interested in finding out how their bodies function, from the digestive system to respiration, the heart, circulation and composition of the blood, the kidneys and the body's waste disposal system, the reproductive system and development of babies. Associated with this the value and composition of various foods, · proteins, carbohydrate and fats, and the importance of vitamins can be looked at.

There are many simple experiments which can be done with the five senses, and the results sometimes come as a revelation for they disclose how easily the senses can be deceived, as well as opening up new vistas. These experiments can lead naturally into work on how the eye, ear and skin work.

Experiments with vision

(1) Close one eye, then hold a pencil in front of the other eye in line with a farther away object such as a porthole. Look hard at the pencil, then at the porthole. This shows how the eye cannot focus on two objects at the same time when they are at different distances – either one or the other is blurred.

(2) Shine a torch into the eyes of another person who has covered her eyes for at least ten seconds. The pupils expand in the dark as they need to receive more light, but shrink in bright light as they need less.

(3) Try to put a pen top on a pen at arm's length with one eye open only. This shows how essential two eyes are for 3-D manipulation.

(4) Draw and colour black a circle of about 1.5 cm (half inch) diameter on a piece of white paper. About 5 cm (2 inches) from the circle draw a cross with 2 cm (1 inch) lines. Shut one eye and hold the paper about 30 cm (12 inches) in front, looking hard at the circle only, but still being able to see the cross. Slowly bring the paper forward. At one point the cross will disappear, demonstrating the eye's blind spot.

(5) Pointing to a faraway object then closing each eye alternatively will show a child which is his master eye. The object will stay in place with the master eye open, but move with the non-master eye.

Experiments with sound

(1) Stretch elastic bands of different sizes and lengths and pluck them to demonstrate how sound is made by vibration and how higher and lower notes are made.

(2) The vibrations in the voice box when sounds are made can be felt by throwing the head back and feeling the throat while a very low and high 'aaah' is sung.

(3) While someone else is talking, cup the ears and move them forwards. This effect can be compared to dogs cocking their ears.

(4) Put cotton wool in one ear and close the eyes. Get someone else to move a ticking watch away and see how far off it can be heard on each side by measuring the cut-off point.

(5) Fill four glasses with different amounts of water and tap the sides with a spoon, to show how different notes are made.

(6) Put a ticking watch (a stopwatch is good for these experiments) on a table. Stand at the other end of the table and listen to the watch (it may not even be audible). Then put an ear to the table. This observation can be developed by similar experiments into discovering how well sound travels through other solids and liquids (without putting the watch in water!).

Experiments with other senses

(1) Smell various substances when blindfolded and try to identify them, e.g. curry powder, vinegar, cut onion, soap, sugar or flour.

(2) Taste some of these substances while blindfolded (maybe not the soap!).

(3) Taste the same substances in a different order, this time blindfolded but with the nose pinched off. Some of the tastes will not be so easily recognised, demonstrating how our sense of smell influences our sense of taste. (The blindfold is to remove the other influence of sight.)

(4) Taste some lemon juice, then eat some sugar, then taste the lemon again. The strong sweet taste makes the lemon juice appear even sharper, showing how tastes can be changed. A similar distortion of taste can be achieved by tasting an apple both before and after a lick of toothpaste.

(5) Fill three mugs with water: hot, cold and tepid. Put fingers of one hand in the cold, the other hand in the hot and then transfer both to the tepid water. This demonstrates the delusion of our sense of touch, the tepid water feeling hotter or cooler depending on which hand one chooses to believe.

(6) Without looking, try to guess when a minute is up on a stopwatch. Most children will guess short of the time. See if one can improve one's guess with a second try.

From experiments such as these children can learn that the senses are unreliable for measuring accurately and therefore see the need for instruments and standard units. Nearly all boats will have a selection of instruments for measuring a variety of phenomena, and the child should be encouraged to use as many of these as possible and to consider the principles involved. It might be interesting to compare results of their own measurements against those of instruments – for example, with a leadline against the depth sounder, or a ribbon streamer in the rigging and compass against the wind direction indicator. Instruments like a thermometer, barometer or simple anemometer can all be used for measurement.

A natural development from experiments with the eye is looking at the behaviour of light with mirrors and lenses. This can lead on to the principles involved in binoculars, telescopes, sextants and cameras, all items that might be available on board a boat. Simple diagrams of these instruments can be drawn showing how the light rays travel through them.

Here Ivan describes how he made a pin hole camera:

> First I got an empty can of mushrooms with one end cut off. Then I made a hole in the other end with a piece of wire. Next I fastened some tracing paper with an elastic band to the cut open end. Then I pointed it at a window and looked into the tracing paper. I saw everything the wrong way round.

How the image of the window becomes upside down is a thought provoking point for a child to consider. A similar inversion is seen by writing one's name on a piece of paper and holding it up to a mirror. By placing two mirrors upright at an angle to each other with a small object such as a toy car between them, and looking with one's eyes level with the surface on which the mirrors and the object are standing, the number of toy cars seen can be altered by altering the angles of the mirrors. An older child can measure these angles with a protractor and draw a diagram. By using mirrors and small beads in this way, patterns similar to those of a kaleidoscope can be made.

After considering light travelling in straight lines, putting a straight stick into a bucket of water can introduce a child to the apparent bending of light rays and the idea of refraction. The way that a lens bends the light rays so that they appear to come from a larger object farther away can also be demonstrated, and the focal point found by moving the position and distance of both eye and object.

Senior level

Expanding some of the ideas in the previous section, the uses and principles of heat, light, machines, electricity and magnetism could be explored, as could the properties of air and water.

The study of substances and their properties can begin with simple experiments to see which substances will dissolve in water and what colour or opacity of solution is formed. A range of easily available substances to be tested are salt, sugar, flour, baking powder (sodium bicarbonate), vitamin C tablets (ascorbic acid) and potassium permanganate. If litmus or indicator papers are available (I scrounged some from a science teacher in Papua New Guinea) the acidity, neutrality or alkalinity can be tested for a range of substances such as vinegar, lemon juice, saltwater, toothpaste, soap powder solution, baking powder, ink, milk, tomato sauce, coffee, whisky and white spirit.

The ways of separating substances can be explored by filtering, i.e. separating a solid such as a suspension of flour in water from the liquid with a funnel and filter paper (coffee filter papers can be used for this). Separation by evaporation can be demonstrated with a small concentrated solution of salt in water, heated in an inverted saucepan lid over a saucepan of boiling water. A further way of separation, by paper chromatography, can be shown by dropping a blob of ink onto blotting paper and adding water slowly drop by drop. This is also a way of demonstrating that ink is not a single substance, black ink revealing the most surprising components.

Work on substances can expand into classification of these substances into solids, liquids and gases, and the conversion of one form to another can be discussed. Other ways of classification, such as making lists of metals and non-metals, can be introduced. A child might also like to consider how many ways he can think of to classify children: hair colour, eye colour, height, weight, shoe size, number of dental fillings or how high each child can jump. Similarly, in the study of living things an older child will be able to proceed to more detailed classifications, such as considering the vertebrates and invertebrates and the characteristics of various classes within the major families. The divisions of the plant world into flowering plants, trees, grasses, seaweeds and so on could also be investigated. Constructing a key for identifying animals or plants can also be fun – using, for example, such identifying features as feathers, hair, fur, scales, wings, fins, number of legs, if the animal breathes air, lays eggs, has hooves or paws.

An older child might also look at the various forms of energy and how they can be changed and converted from one form to another.

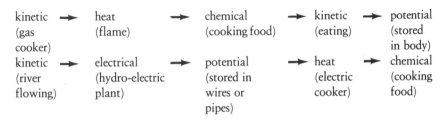

The child might like to consider what energy changes occur in some of the following:

- turning on a torch
- shaking a tin with nails in it
- switching on an electric fan
- pulling down a ball at the end of a rubber band and letting go
- sailing a boat

The conversion of fuel into power and also the use of energy as a means of propulsion will have many practical examples on a boat. The production of electricity on a boat from batteries and the way these are charged can be considered, by running the engine (mechanical use of fuel combustion), wind generator, solar panel (photovoltaic cells), or a towing generator. Neighbouring boats can be exploited here to discover all the alternatives of generating power. Wind propulsion and efficiency using sails, the change of sail angles on different points of sailing, how a windvane selfsteering works, all involve scientific principles and can get an older child thinking and asking questions. Maybe he can even devise his own experiments to find out answers to his questions.

In the bigger and better toyshops, there are many kits available which have been produced specifically for older children with scientific interests. Usually these kits are accompanied by books, which outline experiments to be done. In Australia I bought such a chemistry kit, which came complete with various chemical substances, test tubes, watchglasses, and spatulas. Instead of letting the children play with it indiscriminately, we used it for proper chemistry lessons, carrying out the experiments outlined in the booklet systematically (under my supervision, especially where any heating of test tubes was involved). All these experiments were written up in a format describing exactly what had been done, the result obtained and the conclusions drawn.

Similar kits are available in such fields as electronics and optics, and one can also buy junior microscopes with accessories. All these have accompanying suggestions for their use. The further interests of a scientifically minded child can thus be pursued, although I think it is essential to incorporate the use of these kits into the timetable and so get the full educational value out of them. The older child undoubtedly will have a special interest that may be worth following up in a scientific manner, be it astronomy, navigation or aqua-lung diving with air bottles. A proper study of such subjects should be encouraged, looking closely at the scientific principles involved in both the execution of the activity and the equipment involved. In the case of diving, this understanding of the effects of pressure at different depths and the expansion of nitrogen in the blood and lungs under increased pressure is essential for safety reasons.

The intricacies of astro-navigation using a sextant involve some quite advanced scientific and mathematical concepts, although the young person will see the immediate purpose in the work he does in this field. So often, having a keen interest does produce spectacular results, and the most important parental role at this stage is probably to promote and further a child's own interests. This brings me to the subject of computers, a field where the young appear to be teaching their elders. The proliferation of smaller and cheaper home computers has ensured that this is a subject that will increasingly figure on the educational scene. It is a difficult subject for parents like me whose schooldays lie in the pre-computer age. Yet the manuals that arrive with computers usually explain the basic programming and operation quite well, and the possibilities that the particular model is capable of, once one has mastered its basic language and jargon. But do not be surprised if your offspring lead the way: after all, that is what a voyage into education is all about.

I hope that, by giving a selection of ideas for scientific work that can be carried out without a laboratory, I have shown how science subjects can be tackled afloat. An important aspect is in the scientific recording of the work: firstly by a careful description of what was done, then an accurate report on the results obtained or observations noted, followed by the deduction of a conclusion from the results. In this manner a proper scientific approach is fostered.

18
Skills Worth Acquiring

Teaching a child while cruising will by its very nature result in a personal education, almost in the style of the tutors employed by wealthy families in days gone by. In this framework a child's particular talent or interest can easily be developed as an educational asset. These special interests may cover a wide range of subjects, impossible to discuss in this book, yet the skills needed to pursue these interests successfully are virtually the same for all subjects. Such skills can and should be taught to all children, not only for them to function efficiently later on in whatever job or career they choose, but also to enable them to get full enjoyment and pleasure out of their hobbies and interests.

Basically these skills involve the ability to find and use the information required, and also to be able to assess this information independently. In this era of expanding knowledge, when we cannot know everything, it is important to be able to find out what we want to know as quickly and efficiently as possible.

The first step a child takes in this direction is usually being able to use a dictionary. In the first stages of learning to read and write, a simple picture dictionary can be used, or the child may even compile his own dictionary of new words learnt and spellings needed in his written work. The obvious first requirement is a knowledge of alphabetical order, which can then gradually be developed into considering the alphabetical order of second, third and following letters in a word. Giving a child a list of closely similar words to put into alphabetical order will help develop this skill – for example, shop, shirt, sheet, snow, spot, spell, slow.

Following on naturally from using a dictionary comes the use of an encyclopaedia, which will similarly be arranged in alphabetical order, although a few encyclopaedias are also subdivided into sections or volumes on related topics. These encyclopaedias can be weighty items to carry on a boat, but a good encyclopaedia is essential when following a more personally tailored education and can lessen the need for a lot of other books on different topics. Most encyclopaedias are also published in a junior version, which is less bulky, or alternatively there are small one-volume concise reference books such as Larousse.

Learning to use other reference books will often come about quite naturally as a child asks questions to which a parent does not know the answer. Even if one does know the answer, it may be worthwhile helping the child to find out for himself instead of just telling him if, for example he is identifying stars in the night sky. The first steps are to show a child how to use a table of contents, chapter headings and an index. What use is made of these will depend greatly on what kind of information is required: a simple piece of information, such as the name of Columbus' ship, or a more general area of enquiry, such as how a rainbow is formed.

Although these skills might seem obvious to us as adults, children can be helped greatly to be more proficient in the way they acquire information. They can be taught how to skim quickly through a book or chapter looking for what they want. Having found this, they can be encouraged to read the whole passage for its meaning, not stopping to look up every new word they come across. When they have extracted the gist of the passage, they can go back and look up words if necessary. The ability to extract the essence from a passage and to paraphrase this in one's own words, writing out the main points in a simpler language, is a skill that does require considerable practice. A child can easily be given practice in comprehension, by being asked questions about what he has read, or being asked to summarise a passage in his own words. This kind of work will normally take place in the school programme of reading, writing and language development.

It is also worth teaching a child how to read efficiently. One technique is to skim through the whole material quickly to decide which part is relevant, followed by more attentive reading of that part and the making of notes. Then the section can be reread and revised with the help of the notes to check that no essential point has been missed. Taking notes is also a skill that can be improved by technique and practice, encouraging the child to pick out key points and words. It sometimes helps to note these down in a diagrammatic way, with boxes, circles, arrows between associated ideas or numbered points – in short, any method that aids clarity of thought.

The use of different kinds of books that are organised in different ways should be encouraged, from guidebooks, yearbooks and textbooks to atlases and manuals. When looking for material for a particular project, the use of a variety of books should be emphasised. This may involve combining notes from various sources. The use of footnotes or an appendix can be taught where these occur.

Another essential skill to learn is that of map reading; also the use of charts, atlases and globes. Maps are an abstract symbol, and until a child's concept of spacial layout is sufficiently developed it is not fair to expect him to use a map properly. A young child has to be able to imagine that the views represented are different to his own view of things. This can be encouraged by drawing simple plans of items as seen from above, progressing to drawing a plan of a cabin or boat. When a child can understand what a map represents, then he can progress to using maps and atlases as reference material. This will involve an understanding of what scale is, a knowledge of the points of the compass, the main symbols used and how to locate a place by means of a grid reference. Most sailing children learn to use charts quite quickly, if only to discover where they are or how near the destination is. Motivation is always a great incentive to learning.

From the number of books I write about or recommend – guidebooks, reference books, encyclopaedias – it must seem to some readers that I am trying to turn cruising boats into travelling libraries. It is true that the number of books we carried on our boat did lower the waterline considerably, but I do realise that it is impossible to provide the range of facilities that would be available in a school ashore. This can be partly solved by making use of public libraries in some ports of call to look up things that a child wants to know. When a longer stay in a port is envisaged, it may be possible to join a library and borrow books. If not, most libraries welcome visitors to browse through books on their premises. This is particularly worthwhile when looking up or reading about local history or local affairs. And in some humid tropical places a cool-air conditioned library can be a pleasant place to pass the morning.

A child not only needs to know how to find the information he requires, but should also be able to assess it. Some of the more technical assessment, such as how to interpret data from tables or graphs, will probably be taught in mathematics and the sciences. What is more important is for the child to develop the ability to think independently, to criticise, to discern and to question. These abilities usually only come with a certain maturity, and even some adults appear never to have acquired them. Small children often think parents know everything, and it is sometimes a disillusion for them when they discover that a parent does not have an answer for every question. Older children have a similar awe for the printed word: if it is written in a book it must be right. Pointing out that a particular idea, opinion or theory is only that of the author and can be questioned is a difficult but necessary exercise.

If possible, two different views on a subject should be read, then discussed and commented on. Sometimes this can be done in connection with a past event, such as considering Darwin's theory and the controversy this aroused at the time.

Museums ashore provide plenty of stimulating material. Ivan and Doina imitate the desiccated mummies found in the desert around Nasca in Peru.

Today there are still many theories and ideas that can be examined, for which there is no 'correct' answer and about which there are several schools of thought and conflicting opinions. An interesting exercise is to take a controversial political event and read how newspapers of different political persuasions write about it. Propaganda techniques can be examined and how words are used in different ways to influence us, maybe looking at a selection of advertisements and trying to assess how the advertiser is attempting to get his message across. Obviously this is the kind of work that can only be done with an older child. It is, however, an essential part of education: the ability to debate questions, to form one's own opinion and to be able to back this up with data and argument. It does not matter whether the point at issue is a matter of great political import or just the best way to make bread.

This chapter on acquiring skills may not be very long, but the subject is one of the essential parts in the process of becoming 'educated'. If knowledge is learned and stored facts, then education can be regarded as the process by which one acquires knowledge. A child who has a positive attitude towards gaining the knowledge that he does not yet possess, increases his chance of success. This is why self-motivated children can usually find the information they want quite readily. But to be able to do this, it is necessary also to have learnt the skills involved, to be able to use reference books, indexes and classification keys or read details off a map or chart. It is even better if a child acquires this knowledge by experimentation or first hand from his own experiences. The ability to *learn how to learn* is one of the most important things we can teach a child.

The Finishing Point

In the preceding pages I have dealt with various specific topics concerning cruising with children, from safety to education. In this concluding chapter I would like to discuss some general points, such as the drawbacks and benefits of cruising, and to consider particularly the optimum age for taking children on a longer cruise.

In drawing the threads together, I do not want only to give my own opinion but also to present the views of other parents who have cruised extensively with their children. The people who choose to go cruising are, by the nature of this activity, individuals with independent views as varied as the types of boats they cruise in. Nevertheless, having talked to dozens of cruising families, both during the cruising surveys and while cruising myself, some common opinions did emerge, mainly because similar problems have to be dealt with. However, because of the individuality of cruising folk, there are no universal solutions; something that works well for one family does not for others, and everyone must do what suits them best.

When talking to sailing parents about the problems they have encountered, I have been pleasantly surprised by how few these were; as several parents remarked, only the normal problems that one could meet just as easily on land as at sea. Keeping an eye on active small children is one of the major problems that parents mentioned and one I witnessed on *Abuello III* when I was discussing just this subject with Nina Cadle. During our discussion, her three year old daughter Luisa, who we thought was quietly amusing herself in the forecabin, emerged triumphantly covered from head to toe in baby oil, which she had even massaged into her hair.

The difficulty of finding a babysitter to look after small children was also mentioned by parents, although sometimes a teenager from a nearby boat would oblige. My daughter Doina used to look after one year old Brandi Stocks of *Kleena Kleene II*, not so much for the parents to have a night out, but so they could get on with shopping, provisioning, stowing and the preparation of their boat for a passage without Brandi's help.

Where there were two or more children on a boat who were closer in age, there appeared to be fewer problems of this nature as the children played together and amused themselves. On one boat I came across there was a large age difference between two children, which caused constant friction between the elder sister and much younger brother. Although such problems occur ashore as well, they are sometimes magnified on a boat due to the confined space. The lack of other children, even if it is only to fight and disagree with as well as to play with, does affect the sole child on a boat, and the parents themselves have to be prepared to spend more time amusing a lone child.

Living in the confines of a small boat undoubtedly makes family life a much closer affair than on shore, and as Maria van Zelderen, mother of two teenagers, pointed out, 'It is important to share and talk together about any problems the children may have.' Again this advice is equally valid for life ashore. As Dorine Samuelson of *Swan II* said, 'If the parents are happy and enjoy the sailing life, invariably the children are happy and like it too. However, if one parent is not completely happy, this is often reflected in the children.'

All the older cruising children I spoke to had taken long-term cruising in their stride, although one teenage girl did tend to panic when the weather deteriorated and had to be continually reassured by her parents. Even so, she told me that in spite of the problems she would be happy to go on a cruise again if the chance arose. One sixteen year old boy complained that his parents worried too much about him and would not let him take much part in sailing the boat or go on deck, which made long passages particularly boring. This was unusual, because on most cruising boats with older children on board the parents encouraged their children to become proficient sailors.

Most of the problems, such as the lack of other children and the difficulty of education, affect those on a longer voyage more than those on a weekend sail or a short cruise. For children sailing for shorter periods, the benefits to be gained from cruising far outweigh any of the drawbacks. Even so, the majority of parents I have spoken to, who have undertaken a longer voyage, do consider that the voyage benefited their children in various ways, from learning other languages or making new friends to having their eyes opened to the world around them. Most parents thought that their children were more adaptable, independent and self-reliant than if they had lived ashore. But as one parent remarked, 'There is a price to pay for all benefits.'

After eight years and 90,000 miles of cruising on *White Pointer*, the Zelderens are a good example of how successful family life afloat can be.

Marge Bryson of *Ave del Mar*, who had sailed from Alaska to New Zealand, where I spoke to her, balanced the advantages and disadvantages of the voyage for her twelve year old son Stuart. On the negative side she put the fact that Stuart was living an adult life and that he met few children of his own age. This tended to create a social problem for him, because he had become different to other children and always needed a long time to adjust to being with them again. On the positive side she quoted his self-sufficiency and amazing ability to keep himself amused, as well as the fact that he had learnt that one cannot argue with the forces of Nature. Stuart was way ahead of his age in his schoolwork, a common occurrence among sailing children, but Marge was not sure whether or not it was a good thing for a child to be too precocious. Stuart, who was listening to our conversation, agreed that the lack of friends was the greatest drawback to his cruising life, but one that he was quite willing to accept for the excitement of the voyage.

The Faubert family of the French boat *Kouros* had mixed feelings about the benefits of the voyage for their children. For eleven year old Peggy, the voyage had been an adventure on which she had seen many interesting things, and her parents considered her more sociable and outward looking than she had been on shore. They had grave doubts, however, about the wisdom of taking their son Franklin, then four years old, on a voyage that had already lasted two years, feeling he was too young to appreciate it. They also considered that this had forced him into an adult world too early and had thus affected their relationship with him. Another parent who was very aware of this aspect was Bernard Tournier of *Volte*, who counselled: 'It is so easy for a child to become an adult without ever being a child.' The Tourniers had prepared very carefully for cruising with their two young sons, sailing in gentle stages over a couple of summers and waiting for the children to be a little older before setting off on a world voyage.

It is clear that most parents who embark on a longer cruise have thought long and deep about the whole question of taking their children cruising and the optimum time for doing this. There are differing opinions about the best age at which to take children sailing and, although applying particularly to a longer cruise, some of the arguments are equally valid for weekend and holiday sailing. There are basically two schools of thought: those who think that the younger a child is the better, so that he grows up used to life on board and knows little else, and the contrasting view that older children get far more out of sailing and take a wider interest in a voyage.

Younger children do need a lot of attention and supervision; they can rarely be left to their own devices and have to be amused and played with at sea. In return for the effort expended on them, they do not take that much interest in the voyage and the places visited. Many parents specified to me a minimum age of five for taking a child on an extended cruise, as older children are less trouble and appreciate cruising more. With younger children, however, one does not have the task of education, nor do they miss the company of other children quite so much, being more content to spend most of their time in the family atmosphere.

This lack of contact with other children of a similar age and the difficulty of educating children afloat are the two main drawbacks to cruising with older children. The question of education becomes progressively more difficult as the child gets older. Yet most of the teenage children cruising for long periods told me that they willingly trade these drawbacks for the enjoyment they get out of cruising, both the sailing itself, the places they visit and the style of life. As one sixteen year old put it, 'I've got used to my freedom.'

Susanna Graveleau of *Hispania*, who is a teacher of philosophy by profession, put her finger neatly on the whole question of age. 'It's very easy for parents to mistake what is easier for them as being also better for the child.' Without doubt it is harder work for a parent when a child is very small – arranging different meals, constantly supervising and occupying the child. As a child grows up and becomes more independent, life does become progressively easier for the parent. Yet Susanna considers that in spite of all the rich experiences an older child has, the lack of other children's company and a normal school life is detrimental in the long term. Her son Carlos was aged four when I spoke to her and she thought that this was a good age for cruising.

This dilemma of age does have to be thought out when planning a cruise, especially what one is going to do about the question of education. As André Fily of *Stereden Vor* remarked, 'One should know one's child well, and if that child is not motivated to go cruising, then one should seriously reconsider the idea.' This comment was made in respect of an older child, who would have to show some self-discipline in order to tackle schoolwork afloat. All the older children that I have spoken to had clear opinions on this subject, being quite prepared to deal with the difficulties of studying while cruising.

My own opinion is that the optimum age for a lengthy cruise is between the ages of five and thirteen. From about five years old a child is likely to be able to swim, understand safety rules and have some idea what school consists of. These middle childhood years are also the easiest in which to cope with a child's education, whether by correspondence or by oneself. At this age a child is usually less inhibited about making friends quickly in new places than older children, but old enough to remember details and so gain something permanent and lasting from the cruise. These recommendations are for an extended cruise away from home. For family sailing at weekends and on holidays, the younger a child starts to enjoy sailing the better. Teenagers who have been sailing all their lives and grown up on boats make a most welcome crew for anyone.

Whether one sails for a few weeks or several years, there are many things that children can gain from the sailing life. One of the first things they learn is to be self-reliant and to depend on themselves. Foreseeing the consequences of any action taken soon becomes automatic while sailing, as does a proper regard for possible dangers and a respect for the powerful forces of wind and wave. These factors lead children to gain a degree of self-control, consideration of others, and the ability to look outwards from themselves, all of which help them to become responsible and sensible adults. Many sailing children also acquire an enduring love of the sea, which will remain throughout their lives.

Undoubtedly there are problems and difficulties, but these can all be resolved and overcome if the will to do so is there. Cruising with children is much easier than most people imagine. As Jean-Pierre Martin, cruising for five years with his children on *El Djezair*, told me, 'It's very simple to leave, so one shouldn't look for complications.'

It is not the children who make the problems, but sometimes the parents themselves, who exaggerate the difficulties because they are not prepared to cope with them. This point was brought home to me recently at Heathrow Airport in London, when I was returning eleven year old Fabien Bouteleux to his parents in France after a vacation he had spent with our family. At the waiting point for unaccompanied children, a cluster of adults were fussing around their charges prior to handing them over to the stewardess, making the children nervous and fidgety. Fabien, world traveller that he is with a six year voyage on *Calao* behind

There is a solution for everything, even Christmas in the sunshine.

him, looked on quite relaxed and unperturbed about his impending flight, clearly wondering what all the commotion was about. He showed the confidence and independence that is typical of cruising children.

Children have often accompanied their parents into a new life, as in the days of pioneering or settling new lands, demonstrating their capacity for resourcefulness and adaptability. In many circumstances children have shown that they will take almost anything in their stride, adapt to a new situation or enjoy the adventure of an activity such as sailing. It is the adults who fuss and worry, not the children. Some of these worries are indeed real and parents are right to consider them, but there is nothing that cannot be overcome with a little thought, effort and careful planning. There is absolutely no reason for making the children one's excuse for not going cruising.